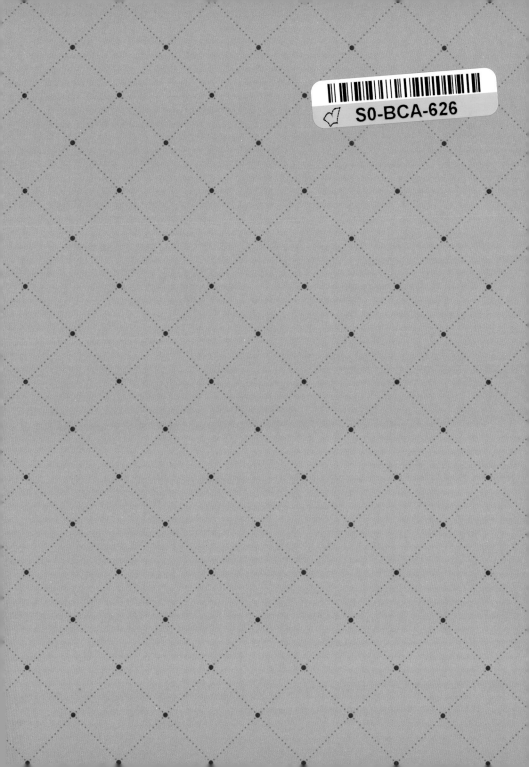

Big decisions often change lives. *Five Bold Choices* will positively inspire you to consider bold choices that could transform your life—and the lives of many others.

—*Tim Pawlenty*, former Governor, State of Minnesota

Adversity brings opportunity, and how we deal with it determines whether we enjoy the journey. *Five Bold Choices* is a great guidebook for anyone who feels stuck and wants to get back on the path they were destined to live.

—*Jerry Colangelo*, Chairman, USA Basketball;
former owner, Phoenix Suns and Arizona Diamondbacks

Most leadership books train readers to share their successes and hide their failures. With stories of remarkable transparency, *Five Bold Choices* helps the reader see failure as not something to fear but an opportunity to grow.

—*Cheryl A. Bachelder*, CEO, Popeyes Louisiana Kitchen, Inc.;
author, *Dare To Serve*

Five Bold Choices blends Jay's riveting personal story with decades of experience as a CEO. The result is a book that gives us the clarity and courage to make the bold choices that make the most out of life's greatest challenges. This book will embolden you to action.

—*Dan Buettner*, *National Geographic* Fellow and three-time
New York Times bestselling author of the *Blue Zones:
Lessons from the World's Longest-Lived People*

This little gem is worth a quick read. You will come away with some solid ideas to make your personal and professional life better.

—*Tad Piper*, retired Chairman and CEO,
Piper Jaffray Companies

Any leader knows that bold choices either bring growth or disaster. Making bold choices wisely is the key. Based on profound personal experiences, Jay and Larry spell out five fundamentals that we all need as leaders, family members, and friends to make wise choices.

—*Brad Hewitt*, CEO, Thrivent Financial

Drawing upon their own professional and personal experiences, Coughlin and Julian not only offer their insights and wisdom as to how one can navigate life's storms with clarity and conviction, but do so while leading the reader on an intimate journey emerging from their own spiritual and personal renewal. Be forewarned: reading this book will not only cause one to reexamine and reassess his or her current status in life, professional or personal, but will provide scriptural principles necessary to pursue a life of influence rather than a life of affluence. Coughlin and Julian use various passages of Scripture to drive home the strategic importance of being grounded and balanced, both spiritually and personally. I recommend *Five Bold Choices* to those individuals who may be re-examining their standing in life or who simply need quiet reassurance that they are on the right path.

—*Dr. Alan Cureton*, President,
University of Northwestern St. Paul, MN

Authentic! Transparent! Powerful! A clear framework that I can personally apply to overcome challenges. Jam-packed with relevant life-changing truth! A huge thanks to Coughlan and Julian for sharing *Five Bold Choices* with the world.

—*David Horsager*, speaker, strategist, and author of *The Trust Edge*

Five Bold Choices

Rise Above Your Circumstances

and Redefine Your Life

Jay Coughlan & Larry Julian

BroadStreet Publishing Group, LLC
Racine, Wisconsin, USA
BroadStreetPublishing.com

Five Bold Choices: Rise Above Your Circumstances and Redefine Your Life

Copyright © 2016 Jay Coughlan and Larry Julian

ISBN-13: 978-1-4245-5314-3 (hardcover)
ISBN-13: 978-1-4245-5315-0 (e-book)

Stock or custom editions of BroadStreet Publishing titles may be purchased in bulk for educational, business, ministry, fundraising, or sales promotional use. For information, please e-mail info@broadstreetpublishing.com.

Cover design by Chris Garborg, GarborgDesign.com
Interior design and typesetting by Katherine Lloyd, theDESKonline.com

Printed in China
16 17 18 19 20 5 4 3 2 1

Dedications

Jay Coughlan

Jule: I delight in your peace and presence, adore your companionship, and treasure your commitment. You are my best choice ever.

Alexa, Derek, and Tyler: You motivated and inspired me to get in balance because, ultimately, you became the actual gauge for appreciating my journey in life.

Mom: Your love and encouragement has meant more to me than you'll ever know.

Dad: Someday I'll get the chance to say, "Thanks. Sorry. Missed You."

Larry Julian

This book is dedicated to
all those who are determined to get up
every time they fall.

Contents

Introduction:
Overcoming Failure—The Portal to Your Success

Introduction:

Overcoming Failure–
The Portal
to Your Success

We believe difficulties and failures

are opportunities and stepping-stones

to a life of significance instead

of obstacles to be avoided.

1

Reclaiming the Life You've Been Called to Lead

(Larry)

There are times in life when we feel stuck. Our noble desire for a successful career and family life gets bogged down or derailed by the challenges before us. Whether it be a difficult circumstance or our own limiting beliefs and fears, we can't seem to get past what holds us back.

We all go through peaks and valleys as we journey through life. Sometimes our valleys are self-inflicted. We make mistakes, some big and some small, and we pay the consequences of our actions. We fail and get down on ourselves. Other times, trials happen through no fault of our own, such as an illness, unexpected death, or inopportune business misfortune. These difficulties can stop us in our tracks.

Then there are other times when we seem to be in between our peaks and valleys, a time when life is okay but not perfect. We know unresolved issues need to be addressed but set them aside because we're busy doing other things. Our job brings security, but it's not fulfilling. We want to be a better spouse and parent, but busyness trumps our priorities.

These times tend to breed avoidance and inaction, and we drift away from fulfilling our potential instead of driving toward it. Regardless of whether we're stopped or drifting, we're stuck in a place we don't want to be and can't seem to get out of it.

I have seen these trying times create defining moments that significantly change the trajectory of people's lives—in both good and bad ways. I've seen people rise to the occasion and use their challenge as a springboard to realizing their full potential, and I've seen others die a slow death of mediocrity. How we respond in these moments is critical. The stories of these people always lead me to the same questions:

- Why do some people have the ability to overcome their greatest challenges while others fall victim to circumstance?

- How do people muster the courage to persevere though the tough issues in their life?

- How do people get unstuck?

The Purpose of This Book

Five Bold Choices is about helping you find (or reclaim) the real life you've been called to lead by helping you break through the barriers that prevent you from realizing your untapped potential.

We believe difficulties and failures are opportunities and stepping-stones to a life of significance instead of obstacles to be avoided. *Five Bold Choices* is based on three principles:

1. The difficulties and failures you avoid and fight are the very portals to your success and significance.

2. You cannot overcome life's challenges on your own. You need a realistic plan, process, and support system of trusted peers and loved ones.

3. Everyone's story matters. Your story of perseverance and overcoming will help you not only realize your potential but also inspire others and leave a lasting impact on those around you.

About the Authors: Two Different Perspectives with One Common Goal

I remember attending a small gathering of board members at a cocktail party the night before I was to give a speech for the National Speakers Association. As I was enjoying a cheese puff, a board member from New York asked me, "So, what gives you the right to speak to our group tomorrow?"

I nearly coughed out my hors d'oeuvre! However, upon reflection, I realized it was a great question. In essence, he was asking the tough questions that come with the privilege of teaching and inspiring others: Who are you? Why should we trust you? What credentials do you have?

These are fair questions worth answering before Jay and I share how we can help you persevere through your challenges to realize your potential. Let me at least start with a brief introduction.

As the author of *God Is My CEO* and a business leadership coach, I've had the privilege of getting inside the hearts and minds of CEOs and business leaders for over twenty-five years. I know what makes a good leader, and, more importantly, I know the leadership landmines that cause even the best leaders to falter. My passion is to share real stories of transparent and authentic leaders and then provide thought-provoking questions so others can find and fulfill their potential.

Jay Coughlan has served as a highly successful CEO of industry leaders such as Lawson Software and XRS Corporation. He was also an up-and-coming business leader with a promising career who was confronted with a personal hell that started with making a terrible choice to drive while intoxicated after drinking at a bar with his dad. This decision resulted in a horrific car crash that killed his dad and left him severely injured both physically and emotionally. Jay survived but faced a living nightmare that included overwhelming guilt, the prospect of a four-year prison sentence for criminal vehicular homicide, and a shattered career, family, and life.

I love the quote that goes, "People don't care how much you know until they know how much you care."[1] Jay and I are writing this book because we care about you and your potential.

First, let me say that Jay and I are complete opposites. We bring entirely different skill sets, careers, and viewpoints to this book. He's had a successful career as a CEO; I've had a successful career as an author and business coach. He's confident; I'm cautious. He'll show you how to achieve your goals; I'll help you discover the "why" behind your goals. He's direct, to the point, and will motivate you to confront your truth and take action; I will help you see your blind spots and encourage small action steps to get you moving toward your goals.

We also have three things in common:

1. We are completely in alignment in our passion to help you persevere to find your potential. There are many portals that can lead to your successful journey. We believe our differing perspectives will provide options for you to consider along the way.

14

2. We know pain, failure, shame, and negative self-talk all too well. We understand the challenges our readers face, so we do our best to respectfully meet you at your particular point of need.

3. We know what it means to overcome and even appreciate the journey in spite of its challenges. We believe you can endure as well, and through that process leave a lasting impact on others along the way. We don't want to insult your intelligence with platitudes of "pie in the sky" hope but give realistic hope of realizing your full potential.

And we believe our differing styles and vantage points provide the ideal process to help you get unstuck.

How This Book Will Help You

Jay will show you how to get from point A to point B. He'll introduce the five bold choices that worked for him: clarity, accountability, adaptability, confidence, and balance. These principles have been widely used in leadership development for years, but it's one thing to learn them and quite another to boldly live them through your choices and actions.

In each chapter, Jay will share how each choice helped him on his four-year journey from convicted felon to successful CEO. While he is compassionate, his advice will be direct, to the point, and brutally honest. He is a "get it done" kind of guy. Trust me when I say he has the ability to move people to action. If I know one thing about Jay, it's that he's big on accountability.

After he shares his practical advice, I will supplement his thoughts with commentary from a wide range of leaders, which I've taken from my books and coaching practice.

Final Thoughts

On the surface, business leaders genuinely seek to grow their business and their capacity as leaders. However, behind almost every business problem lies a deeper internal struggle. I've found people in all positions, from CEO to line employees, wrestling with challenging dilemmas and trying to make sense of situations that have no simple solutions. These are talented people who want to make a difference but are stuck for one reason or another.

At the core, they want meaning and purpose in their work, they seek clarity and direction in the midst of their confusion, and they desire a solution to the constant struggle to balance work and family. They want to live out their faith at work but feel constrained within a diverse business culture. Most struggle alone with these issues, and alone is not a good place to be. Rarely have I found that business leaders fail because of their core competencies. More often than not, they fail because they can't bring themselves to confront and overcome the nagging issues head-on.

As an author, coach, and mentor, my role is to draw out the truth of situations and expose the lies we often tell ourselves. My role in this book is to be your coach, advocate, and cheerleader. For me, the most powerful way to do that is through true stories of transparent leaders who risk being vulnerable to share the real story behind their public persona—the times when faith trumped fear, humility took precedence over pride, and serving others superseded self-serving.

One last note before I introduce Jay to share his story. Clearly, it's unique and dramatic—the kind of story Hollywood loves. Superficially, it seems like an entertaining rags-to-riches tale of a shameful convicted felon who finds his faith and turns his life around to become a successful

CEO. This is true, but there's so much more to it. He gets to the core of what we all struggle with: overcoming guilt and fear, confronting the challenges we avoid, and persevering despite the constant barrage of obstacles we face daily.

Regardless of where you are in life, I think you'll find Jay's experience both inspiring and practical. For some, it will be a faith story—one of redemption, forgiveness, and a second chance. For others, it will be a practical manual for any business leader, entrepreneur, or organization that seeks a solid business plan and process in the midst of turbulent times. Or perhaps it will be both. However you want to view Jay's story, we believe this book can help you persevere and appreciate the journey along the way.

2

Forgiven by God but Not the State

(Jay)

Here is my story, as shared in Larry's book *God Is My Success: Transforming Adversity into Your Destiny*:

It was just getting dark. My dad and I were having a great time hunting together and drinking, but it was time to get home. I was racing home with my dad to get back in time for my son's third birthday party.

The next thing I remember was waking up in excruciating pain. I had a neck brace on and was lying on a gurney in an ambulance. I could hear the paramedic saying, "No . . . can't deal with this kind of injury . . . gotta go to Hennepin County!"

The next time I woke up, I looked up and saw all these bright lights with a lot of people running around. My mom and my wife, Jule, were standing over me. The only thing I knew was that I was in a lot of pain.

Each move was a huge deal. Apparently I had shattered my hip. I also remember saying, "That really hurts," when the doctor moved my hand.

I saw the expression on my mom's face and knew something was terribly wrong. Mom looked at me and softly said, "Your dad didn't make it." My dad died. As I put the pieces together that we had been in an accident, somehow, I came to the realization that I had done it—I killed my dad. I remember letting out a scream and crying and trying to rip myself out of the bed I was strapped down on. I didn't know where I thought I was going, because I couldn't walk or even move. I was just trying to leave. I was at an ugly place. I wanted to run somewhere, to go somewhere, to get away from the pain…

Then the physical pain stopped. Taking its place was an emotional pain. It was ten times worse. I dreamed that I had killed my dad and nothing else mattered. I screamed in agony.

I woke up and realized that the nightmare was real. I was just in a world of hurt—in a drug-induced haze with an empty pit in my stomach. I was in a nightmare, awake. I was lying alone in a hospital room, and there was this clock with big black numbers on the wall at the end of my bed. I remember staring at the red second hand as it went around the dial. I held a dispenser in my right hand that dispensed morphine. It was supposed to help with the pain, but the pain never went away. I kept going in and out of consciousness. I looked up at the clock and then closed my eyes. I had these terrible, terrible dreams. I don't even know how to describe them because they were so bizarre and ugly. Then I woke up soaking wet from perspiration. It felt like four or five hours had gone by. It had only been three minutes.

I didn't care about anything. I have a wife and three kids. They never came to my mind once, and they're as important to me as anything.

I could see my wife talking to me, but I couldn't hear her. I couldn't hear my mom. I couldn't hear the clergy who came to talk to me. Whatever they were saying, I couldn't hear it. I just remember knowing I was responsible for killing my dad. My dad, my best friend, who I called every week for the last fifteen years, wasn't there—because I killed him. That's all I remembered. That's all I focused on.

I lived in my nightmare until one afternoon when a stranger walked into my hospital room. I don't remember why this guy showed up, how he showed up, or who he was. I'd never met him before. I thought, "Why are you here?" but I didn't bother asking. We started talking, and sooner or later he asked, "Are you seeking Jesus?" I angrily snapped back, "I don't know what you're talking about. I'm hooked up to these machines and I killed my dad!" He talked about forgiveness and admitting that I was a sinner. I thought, "I'm at the top of the sinner list, because I was drinking and driving and I killed my dad."

Then he said, "If you want to receive forgiveness, you have to accept that you have sinned and ask the Lord for forgiveness." I don't know if our conversation lasted two minutes or twenty minutes, but I found myself praying with this stranger, asking Jesus into my life. All I know is that after the man left I felt a whole lot better. Shortly after, Jule, who thought I was mentally gone, walked into the room. I was sitting up in bed. I looked at her and said, "I just accepted Jesus into my life." Jule said that I was a completely different person when she saw me.

It was a powerful moment, but it wasn't like "BOOM," being hit by a lightning bolt. But the guilt was gone, so much that I could see. I was forgiven and I didn't deserve it. Things started to get better from there. Until then, I had only remembered the clock and my bad dreams. I started to get my memory back. The next day I decided to go off the morphine. I wasn't supposed to go off it for another week, but the pain had subsided enough to stop it.

I still missed my father, and I was still accountable for his death, but I had forgiveness and didn't have the guilt associated with it. I had a second chance at everything and life looked different. I remember turning to Jule and saying, "Let's go." I wanted to get out of the hospital and start my life again.

My life back home was upside-down. Our house was transformed into a medical facility. The dining room was my hospital room. It was a bit crazy, but it was great to be out of the hospital and back in my own home. I had been in a wheelchair, recovering for three months, when I got the letter I knew was coming. I opened the letter and read the words: *criminal vehicular homicide—four-year prison sentence.* I was forgiven by God, but not the state.

The prospect of serving a four-year jail sentence brought an awful sense of dread to me and my wife. As we began to prepare for our trial, the anxiety and worry began to grow. My meetings with my lawyer were strained. My lawyer tried to build a defense by stating the condition of the road, but I told him, "Look, I was drunk. I missed the turn and hit the train. I killed my dad! The only way we're going to do this is to talk about me being accountable."

The stress was growing with each passing day. Every day I woke up thinking, "Is this nightmare ever going to be over?" We were in a system we didn't know anything about. I was guilty. And if I was found guilty, I'd be penalized and it would ruin my life. The best-case scenario was that I'd have no income for two years. The worst case was four years. In the back of my mind I was thinking, "I'm going to lose my house. What will my family do? It's over!"[1]

The Story behind the Story: Jay's Comments Eighteen Years Later

I've been asked by Larry and many others, "Why do you want to write this book eighteen years after the accident?"

I've been speaking to groups and sharing my story ever since my crash, conviction, and recovery. My talk details my journey, and the audiences have ranged from faith-based groups to business leaders. The faith-based groups want to hear how God transformed my life and gave me a second chance on life, while the business groups want to know how I went from convict to successful CEO in just four years, taking Lawson Software public and achieving the fifth-largest initial public offering (IPO) in Minnesota history.

After each talk, people line up to speak with to me. Because I'm so transparent in sharing my thoughts, they open up to me as if my vulnerability gives them permission to share the true feelings they've kept bottled up for a long time. I hear comments like, "I'm not where I want to be in life. I want more out of life," "I'm in midlife (or midcareer) crisis," and "Man, I'm just tired. How come I'm so worn out?" I've observed so many people who are frustrated, worried, and discouraged, and I've come to the conclusion that people, men in particular, are stuck.

People ask, "How is it that you were so successful considering the dire circumstances you went through over a long period of time?" I answer, "I've had success, but I'm also a convicted felon. In the midst of a skyrocketing career, I went to jail. What does success really mean? For me it was about perseverance. It's really not about success. Success is fleeting."

There are two things I know about success. First, I've yet to meet anyone who is successful at everything they do. I've met a lot of people who are successful in business yet struggling with something in their family or personal life. Second, like the famous Clint Eastwood line in the movie *Unforgiven*, "Deserve's got nothing to do with it."[2] It doesn't mean that just because we're working hard, we're going to be successful. There are too many variables we can't control. It's about persevering and finding our potential along the way. Potential is really about how we act and enjoy the journey through life.

It doesn't matter whether guys have faith or not; they just want to know how I persevered. They're constantly asking me, "How did you do it?" I say, "Faith," and they respond, "Okay, great! What else?" or "I prayed this morning. What do I do next?" So I had to go back and figure out what it was, in addition to my faith, that gave me the ability to get through. As I reviewed the last eighteen years, I discovered that while my faith played a huge role, there were defining moments that required a bold choice that helped me endure the worst times and find my true potential in the process.

As you go through this book, Larry and I will introduce five critical areas—clarity, accountability, adaptability, confidence, and balance—that can be stepping-stones on your journey. Each of these areas required decisions that defined my life and enabled me to appreciate the journey. It is my hope and prayer that this book will inspire you to make bold choices that will define your life.

Life's challenges demand your response,

and that response defines your character

and determines your destiny.

Difficulty is an essential part of our story.

It calls us to overcome, persevere,

and share our story to inspire others.

3

The Ugly Truth versus the Beautiful Lie

(Larry)

Jay didn't allow the failures and mistakes of his past define him. Through the grace of God, he was given a second chance, but the road to recovery didn't come easy. It required hard work, determination, and perseverance. It entailed confronting the ugly truth versus the beautiful lie. It meant choosing the harder right path over the easier wrong one.

In the movie *A Few Good Men* with Tom Cruise and Jack Nicholson, there is a climactic courtroom scene where the lawyer played by Tom Cruise demands, "I want the truth!" Jack Nicholson, sitting on the witness stand, snaps back, "You can't handle the truth!"[1] What a profound statement.

By nature, humans are inclined toward ease, comfort, and security.

We are motivated by immediate gratification and avoidance of pain. Who wouldn't be? I'm the first to admit that I love my comfort zone. I'm the anti-salmon, preferring to float down a river instead of swim upstream.

Sigmund Freud's pleasure principle states that humans seek pleasure and avoid pain. I'm not here to slam the advertising and marketing world, but we've seen this principle in advertising from our earliest childhood. Let's be honest. How many times have you heard phrases like "easy three-step process," "guaranteed or your money back," "boatloads of cash," or "lose fifteen pounds in just two weeks"? It's because by nature and calculated design many of us prefer the beautiful lie over the ugly truth. Most people want something that offers pleasure and satisfaction without the pain, effort, risk, and sacrifice associated with achieving a desired goal.

I wish there were a simple answer, a three-step formula, or a handy tip sheet to remedy your pain or eliminate your difficulty, but quite honestly, that wouldn't resolve the real issue. Life's challenges demand your response, and that response defines your character and determines your destiny. Difficulty is an essential part of our story. It calls us to overcome, persevere, and share our story to inspire others.

We all reach turning points that define

the direction of our lives—some big but

mostly small. The bold choices we make

today lead to a better tomorrow.

4

Channeling Your Inner Rocky: Choosing the Harder Right over the Easier Wrong

(Larry)

Every year in January, millions of people make New Year's resolutions only to give them up by mid-February. Chances are good that you've probably experienced this phenomenon firsthand. Now, are you ready for my one reason why people give up? Wait for it … *it's hard to do*. In all seriousness, there are many reasons we quit, but, at the risk of sounding simplistic, the main one is that it's difficult to sustain doing the harder right thing over time. It's so much easier to quit.

However you define your situation, whether it's being stuck, out of balance, or in the midst of a major crisis, Jay and I recognize that rising above your difficulty and getting back on track requires not just action but courageous action—bold choices that require wisdom, patience, determination, and perseverance. This type of action, while not easy, can bring life-changing results.

To clarify "courageous" a bit further, I'm not suggesting the Hollywood courage of Charlton Heston playing Moses parting the Red Sea or Rocky Balboa going fifteen rounds with Apollo Creed. I'm talking about the everyday moral courage of choosing the harder right path over the easier wrong one through small acts of bravery and persistence each day.

Defining Moments

A good story includes certain basics: a plot, characters, and scenes in which the story unfolds. The most significant element is the turning point (or crisis point) when the main character faces a critical moment involving a decisive change for the better or worse. As an example, if we go back to the movie *Rocky*, the turning point came in the scene before the big fight.

Rocky returns home to Adrian late at night, after a long walk during which he tried to psyche himself up for his big boxing match with Apollo Creed the next morning. Adrian sees the worry on Rocky's face and asks him what's wrong. In a moment of complete vulnerability, he shares his deep inner thoughts of self-doubt, fear, and lack of confidence. Rocky has reached his crisis point—he'll either quit and go back to being the loser that everyone has said he is, or he'll gather the courage to do his best fighting a powerful foe.

This turning point sets up the final scene, which is the fight with the champion, Apollo Creed. As most know, Rocky fights the champ and gives everything he has, going all fifteen rounds until the final bell rings.

While Apollo Creed wins the fight, the hero and true champ is Rocky because he overcame his fears and courageously did his best.

People love stories like this because they see themselves in Rocky. They find the inspiration that they too can overcome their fears and go the distance with the giant foes in their ring of life. However, it's one thing to live out your thoughts in a movie and quite another to live courageously and take action in real life. Persevering in real life requires bold choices to walk the harder right path instead of the easier shortcut.

We all have defining moments in our life. Some are big life-changing moments, such as when we decide to propose marriage, choose a career path, or desire to start a family. But I believe it's the thousands of small yet bold choices that define our lives.

I experienced a significant defining moment when I married my wife, Sherri, but it has been the many small but bold choices to love and persevere during the rough patches that have defined our marriage. I also made a life-changing decision to become a follower of Jesus, but it's been the thousands of small decisions to walk by faith during times when it seemed risky and counterintuitive that have strengthened my relationship with him.

Almost twenty years ago, Jay made an important decision to not let personal tragedy define his life. He then made one bold choice after another as he endured a roller-coaster journey one crisis at a time.

Let's be honest. It's easy to get angry and much harder to be patient. It's easy to be self-serving and harder to sacrifice. It's easy to fall in love but harder to love unconditionally. It's easy to make resolutions but hard to change a lifestyle.

The greatest gift we've all been given is the freedom to choose. We all reach turning points that define the direction of our lives—some big but mostly small. The bold choices we make today lead to a better tomorrow.

Jay and I wholeheartedly believe that regardless of your situation, you've been given the capacity to overcome whatever obstacles you face. It will take hard work on your part, but the return on investment will be significant. We urge you to seek the truth and eschew the lies—to choose the harder right path over the easier wrong one. These bold choices will define your life and help you appreciate the journey to becoming what God has destined you to be.

Discussion Guide

- What's your reaction to Jay's story? What insights have you gained?

- In what area of your life do you feel stuck?

- Describe a defining moment in your past that changed the trajectory of your life?

- In the introduction we share that the difficulties you avoid are the portals to your significance. What's your response to this statement?

- What bold choice can you make to move yourself closer to your better tomorrow?

Bold Choice 1:

Clarity

Keeping the Important Things

Important

Diligent work is a good thing,

but we must discern when it becomes

a distraction from what really matters.

5

The Burden
of Busyness

(Larry)

Phil Styrlund, CEO of The Summit Group, was the epitome of the successful businessman who was busy traveling the world, growing a successful sales training company. Years later he shared this story that helped me distinguish between being busy and being relevant:

In 2009, I had just bought a business, my mom passed away, and the economy evaporated. I was out there grinding away in order to pay the bills. It was an extremely busy and draining time period in my life. I wore myself down. I was mentally and spiritually exhausted; stopped in my tracks. Up to that point I thought I could out-solve and out-work any problem. It literally brought me to my knees. I was brought to a place of utter and complete dependence on God. Any pride and hubris I had was stripped away. This "great humbling" helped me divest myself of lesser activities and invest in things that mattered. As C. S. Lewis said, "to major in the majors, not major in the minors." I found that to gain knowledge was to accumulate, yet build wisdom is to eliminate. It's the only cure to the activity addiction.[1]

I've always appreciated Phil's authenticity in revealing that, to some degree, our pride can drive our busyness beyond what's important. Diligent work is a good thing, but we must discern when it becomes a distraction from what really matters.

As described in Phil's story, we are all susceptible to falling into this trap. Busyness can drain your energy to the point of physical, emotional, and spiritual exhaustion. In the next chapter, Jay will share how goal-setting and energy-replenishing strategies can help you find clarity.

To find clarity, you need to know

your starting point and where

you're going, and have an honest

awareness of the obstacles in your way.

In order for you to find your potential,

you'll need to prioritize.

6

Getting Laser-Focused on the Things That Matter Most

(Jay)

Winston Churchill provides a great quote that sums up the reality behind the clarity we seek: "You will never reach your destination if you stop and throw stones at every dog that barks."[1]

In almost every one of my coaching sessions, the participant starts off by telling me how busy he is. Bottom line, we're all busy. We wear busyness like a badge of honor. Go to any neighborhood party, restaurant, or office water cooler and listen to what they say. Everyone will share how busy they are with kids, work, travel, family, and other commitments. But are they achieving anything? One of the first questions I ask is, "What do you want to do?" It's amazing how many people can't even answer the question.

John Wooden, the famous UCLA basketball coach, once said, "Don't mistake activity with achievement."[2] How about you? Are you achieving anything? How do you prioritize all the demands before you? How do you prioritize your days, weeks, and months?

To find clarity, you need to know your starting point and where you're going, and have an honest awareness of the obstacles in your way. In order for you to find your potential, you'll need to prioritize. Put all the things you do in order of importance. I challenge you to sort through the busyness of your life and gain a clear focus on the things that really matter. Identify and prioritize issues of substance that are relevant, meaningful, and significant. By doing so, you'll be better able to discern the noise of every distraction that barks for your attention.

Energy as the Fuel for Your Journey

Imagine that we're preparing for a cross-country car trip from New York to California. While there are many ways of mapping out our journey, packing, and making those final preparations, there's one essential element that is common to all: we need energy. We don't gas up once in New York and drive all the way to California; we need to refuel many times throughout the trip.

In the same way, our next step in gaining clarity for our journey is to know not just what provides us energy but what drains our energy. Where do you get your energy? What activities help you gain energy? What kind of people give you energy? What people suck the life out of you? These are critical questions to reflect upon.

As the CEO of a publicly held company, I had to communicate

regularly with our shareholders and investors. I remember dealing with a major shareholder who was a hard-driving type-A major investor. Because he was on the board and a major shareholder, he had immediate access to each quarter's financial performance. If the quarter ended at midnight, he'd be on the phone at 12:01 a.m., wanting to know how we did.

One time right after our third quarter ended, he relentlessly called to find out how that quarter went, leaving phone messages and sending text messages and e-mails. I was in the midst of wrapping up the quarter and heading out for vacation in Montana, so I told my CFO, "We had a great quarter. Just send him all the information." As I was driving to Montana and trying to unwind, I received a one-sentence text from my board member: *Going to be down quarter-over-quarter?* which is a nice way of saying, *You did a good job, Jay. Are you going to be down next quarter?*

This interaction sucked the energy out of me, so I had to make sure I engaged in energy-building activities. Going to Montana was an energy-building activity. I could have allowed my board member's comments to undermine my energy-building trip, but I made a conscious effort not to let that happen. Instead I focused on making my trip an energy-building experience.

Do you know what your energy-building activities are? Who are your energy-building friends? To persevere, you have to figure out where you're going to get your energy. For me it's bike riding, being with family, going to restaurants with friends and family, and hunting. What about you? Start thinking about all the energy-building activities and relationships that help you on your journey.

In addition, take a long look in the mirror and ask yourself what kind of person you are to others. For me, it's important to build intentional energy-giving activities into my life. For example, I enjoy having lunch with others; it gives me an opportunity to listen to people, understand their challenges, and offer encouragement.

Are you an energy-giving or energy-sucking person? You reap what you sow. If you're looking for energy-giving people, give energy to others. At the same time, be aware of your energy level as well as your energy-giving actions toward others, because you can't give energy if you don't have it. Be generous with your encouragement of others. Find ways to fill your bucket so your energy can overflow into others' lives.

Goal Setting as the Key to Clarity and Focus

Simply put, lack of clarity is the number one reason why people quit a job or some major endeavor. It's easy to quit when you have no compelling vision of success and lots of busyness with no direction.

For me, goal setting was the key to clarity and focus. I'd love to tell you I set goals for altruistic reasons, but I didn't. When I was in my early twenties, I was motivated by the almighty dollar, focused on how I could make the most money. In the early 1980s I read an article about a Yale University study on creating wealth. Their study of a graduating class in the late 1950s determined that 5 percent of the class had created more wealth than the other 95 percent combined. I assumed that those who went to Yale in the 1950s looked and acted a lot alike. They were probably white males coming from an educated background. So if all the demographics were similar, what allowed 5 percent of them to create more wealth than the other 95 percent? The answer was shockingly simple: they wrote down their goals. From that point forward I started to write down my goals. Eventually, I learned how to make them specific, measurable, attainable, relevant, and timely (SMART).

This process helped me understand

that it was about more than just

achieving goals; it was about putting

things in the proper perspective

and enjoying the journey along the way.

The process was invaluable. I started getting answers to the tough questions: Where am I going with my career? Where do I want to be in five years? I wrote, *I'm going to be a CEO by the time I'm forty*, and not because I wanted a big leadership role but because CEOs made the most money.

Writing down this goal was a huge motivator. It forced me to ask more questions: What skill set do I need to get where I want to go? What do I need to change? What price am I willing to pay? The process helped me focus on my goals and provided a means for making the tough choices that moved me closer to my goal of becoming a CEO by forty years of age. Every quarter I looked at my goals, tracked and managed them, and advanced.

Goals Change, but Goal Setting Remains the Same

I was on a fast track to achieving my goals at Lawson Software until that fateful day, January 3, 1998, when I had the accident that changed my life forever. Six months after my accident, I looked back on what my goals had been on January 1, 1998. With regard to my faith, I'd written near the bottom of the page, *Number 10 Spiritual: I need to go to church more often because my children need the guidance.*

At thirty-eight, not only was I derailed from my goal of being a CEO by forty, but my goals changed dramatically. First, my faith was moved to the number one spot, and my family moved up to number two. Second, the goals of fighting for my personal and professional life took center stage. In reality, even though I failed and ended up going to jail, I still had my goals. They changed dramatically, but the goal-setting process remained the same. I knew that once I got out of the hospital and broke through the fog, I had to get back on track. I knew where I was, and I knew what I wanted and what I had to do to get there. I asked myself the tough questions and relentlessly worked on my goals during the most challenging four-year process of my life.

Looking back, this process helped me understand that it was about more than just achieving goals; it was about putting things in the proper perspective and enjoying the journey along the way.

The circumstances we face are
very real obstacles that keep us stuck,
but that's not the issue. The true issue
lies in our response in the midst
of our circumstances.

7

It's Not What Happens but What Happens to What Happens

(Larry)

For most people, clarity and goal setting is nothing new. On paper it makes perfect sense. Unfortunately, we don't live our lives on paper. We live in a constantly changing environment with shifting targets and unceasing distractions.

I've found there are two distinct types of leaders when it comes to clarity and achieving goals. The first type, intentional leaders, are focused in their goal setting. They love to set annual, monthly, weekly, and daily goals. Jay certainly falls into this camp. The second type, improvisational leaders, don't like being constrained by goals and prefer to improvise to meet the challenges of the moment. They love the spontaneity and flexibility of their days. They may not be goal setters like Jay, but they can still be focused on their overarching goal.

As an example, Jay's daughter is a medical resident who recently graduated from Georgetown University Medical School. As Jay has shared, "She doesn't write her goals down, but she is laser-beam focused on becoming a doctor."

There is no set formula, only the formula that works for you. Regardless of your unique design, it's still important to sift through the busyness and focus on what's important to you.

The distinction of Jay's story doesn't lie in the achievement of his goals but in the journey itself. Jay, in the midst of a storm of one obstacle after another, developed a clarity and focus on what was most important to him. He didn't allow the obstacles and distractions associated with his dire circumstances to keep him from recovering and rebuilding his life. His story and message, while dramatic, is extremely relevant to most business leaders in today's rapidly changing complex world.

Jay and I find people in all positions, from CEOs to line employees, who are wrestling with dilemmas and trying to make sense of situations that have no simple solutions. Here are a few comments we hear on a regular basis:

- "I've been trying to pursue a ... opportunities. My financial reserves are getting low. Should I abandon my passion and just get a job to pay the bills?"

- "I'm retiring in a few years. I still need to work to feel secure in my retirement, but I feel compelled to serve others in some way. I have no idea what to do."

- "I'm completely worn out! I've tried so hard to be the best provider, dad, and husband but feel like I'm falling short. When I come home after work, there's nothing in the tank for my family."

- "I'm way overcommitted at work, and my travel schedule keeps me away from my family. I've just learned that my son has gotten into trouble at home. The next three months are make-or-break time at our division. I feel compelled to be with my son. What should I do?"

- "My marriage is struggling, yet my wife and I are so busy that we can't find time to work on our relationship. I want to rebuild my marriage but don't know where to start."

Phil Styrlund summed up this lack of clarity issue perfectly: "As I travel about the planet, I see the number one issue is uncertainty. So many leaders are struggling to run a business in the midst of conflict, chaos and complexity. It's like they're choking on one big ambiguity hairball!"[1]

The circumstances we face are very real obstacles that keep us stuck, but that's not the issue. The true issue lies in our response in the midst of our circumstances. When in difficult or frustrating circumstances, we're at risk of making poor decisions. Things are on the line, but we're often not at our best when we most need to be at our best. Clarity is generally defined as clearness of thought or having a clear vision of the outcome. In turbulent times our thoughts can be clouded by anxiety. We develop feelings of inadequacy, and our denial of hard reality creates blind spots that hinder the clarity we seek.

These painful responses aren't relegated to weak-minded people;

rather, they happen to the best and brightest business leaders of our day. One of the most memorable speaking engagements I ever had came on October 24, 2008. That morning, I spoke to one hundred business leaders in New Canaan, Connecticut, a suburb outside New York City. All were wealthy CEOs, business leaders, and stock brokers, of which one-third worked on Wall Street. I was speaking on my recently released book, *God Is My Coach: Finding Clarity in an Uncertain World*, and in the previous weeks the stock market had seen three consecutive weeks of five-hundred-plus point drops, creating the biggest financial crisis since the Wall Street crash in 1929.

These circumstances directly affected this group, so I decided to have the audience fill out a half-page sheet of paper with two simple questions:

What is your response to this recent financial crisis?

What are you going to do about it?

All the participants feverishly wrote out their responses and handed them in. I promptly stuffed the responses in my briefcase and went on with my speech. Later that morning, on my train ride back to New York City, I decided to read the responses.

The comments astonished me. Quite honestly, I was aghast at the crazy thinking coming from some of these executives. ~~tions. Irrational~~ responses. I actually ~~sweat as~~ I read through the answers. One gentleman was devising a scheme to divorce his wife so they could protect his family's financial assets. Another gentleman, living in one of the richest communities in the world with significant possessions, lamented as if he were poor. The saddest answer came from a gentleman who was in obvious despair; he believed his "life was over" because of his financial situation.

I share this story to drive home a crucial point. While our circumstances are legitimate, it's our response that really matters. The real danger lies within. Ralph Waldo Emerson stated it perfectly when he said, "The wise man in the storm prays God not for safety from danger but for deliverance from fear."[2] It is the storm within that endangers him, not the storm without.

As my mentor, Monty Sholund, used to say, "It's not what happens, but what happens to what happens." You might be in a turbulent whitewater time as dire as the one Jay was in, fighting for his personal and professional life, or you might find yourself in a calm but stagnant eddy of life, dealing with a nagging problem that keeps you stuck. Regardless of your situation, your response is critical. Embracing the tough realities and gaining clarity on what matters most is a great starting point on your journey to realizing your full potential.

Keep the Important Things Important

In my opinion, one of the best leadership examples of clarity is that of S. Truett Cathy, the founder of Chick-fil-A. I had the pleasure of interviewing him for my first book, *God Is My CEO,* several years ago. When I visited him at his Atlanta headquarters, I was expecting a stereotypical CEO of a major company, but what I found was a simple man who was crystal clear on what was important to him. His focus made him very successful in business and in life.

Truett lived his life on a simple principle: Keep the important things in life important. He told people that success is not defined in only one area of life but in several. "We have to ask ourselves what's really important," he said. "I have seen people who were very successful in business but a total flop in relationships with their family and the other important things in life. I have seen many fathers who loved their children and were anxious to give them the material things they never had as a child, but failed to give them what's really important. For me, the most important thing is my relationship with the Lord and to live my life as a role model for my children. It's nice to have the material things that go with what people generally classify as 'business success'—the nice home and nice cars. All that is secondary when it comes to my family."[3] On another occasion, he pointed out, "When I was growing up, Sunday was an important day for family times together. For the last fifty-four years, I've accepted that as a principle and have honored God doing it."[4]

Understanding Truett's priorities in life clarified his decision to keep all his restaurants closed on Sunday. Now, Sunday is traditionally the third-most-active day for restaurant sales, generating approximately 14 percent of weekly and annual business. Roughly $50 billion will be spent in restaurants on Sundays, but none of it will be spent in a Chick-fil-A. Not only does this translate into lost revenue potential, but it also means Truett had to deal with the considerable pressure that came from mall operators around the world who wanted Chick-fil-A to be open to feed their customers. That's pressure! But while Truett has had considerable external pressure from ~~the~~ never felt ~~the principles that drove~~ ~~personal and~~ professional life took precedence over the pressures of business.[5]

Jay Coughlan and Truett Cathy are worlds apart in so many ways. Truett was a Southern boy who grew ~~~~ grew up outside Philadelphia. However, they had one thing in common: They were very clear on what was important to them and never wavered from that goal. Neither succumbed to the busyness and demands of outside influences, even when the pressure was great. As CEOs they both experienced circumstances but never let complexity cloud their clarity.

He put forth a clear plan

and persevered through every

obstacle that got in his way.

8

Finding Clarity in the Chaos

(Larry)

Having clarity and prioritizing our goals are important first steps on our journey to a more balanced and abundant life. We can all agree that the busyness and difficult, uncertain circumstances in our lives threaten to derail us from realizing our potential. As well, we know that we need energy to persevere and overcome the external and internal storms in our life.

A crisis is generally defined as a crucial turning point for the better or the worse. It's also defined as a point in a story when the conflict reaches its highest tension and must be resolved. In essence, a crisis is a decision. It comes from the Latin word *krisis*, meaning "to decide."

In the midst of a severe crisis, Jay made a crucial decision when he said, "I won't let this accident define my life." He resolved to save his life, his family, and his career. He put forth a clear plan and persevered through every obstacle that got in his way. His plan included a deliberate reliance on a positive energy source in the form of physical, mental, and spiritual power. This energy gave him the stamina, resilience, and moral strength to withstand all the energy-sucking obstacles that can cause discouragement, despair, and even depression. He knew what he wanted and what he needed.

Based on the gravity of Jay's situation, his story could easily have had a very different outcome. Many people have faced challenges far less serious than Jay's but become victims of their circumstances—or worse, victims of their own negative thinking. That's why having the courage to answer the tough questions in a crisis is so crucial to finding your potential.

One of the things I admire most about Jay is his ability to ask himself those questions in order to get at the most relevant and meaningful issues. This is especially difficult when we're busy battling the pressing challenges before us, and there are few things more challenging than being a convicted felon. As Jay shared, "Having a felony on your record is a bad thing. You lose rights and privileges that others take for granted. Things like driving a car, flying, voting, and applying for a job." Jay was literally fighting to get his life back, and while it was a scary time, he maintained his focus to gain clarity on what mattered most.

How about you? Do you know what you want? Do you know what you need? Are the obstacles you face as big as you think, or have they been exaggerated by your faulty thinking? We recommend you take the time to honestly complete the questions in this chapter's discussion guide. Your answers will set important markers for your journey.

We leave you with a quote from a favorite scene from the movie

Apollo 13. There's a vital scene at the end of the movie when the damaged Apollo 13 rocket is about to reenter the earth's atmosphere on its journey back to earth. Because the rocket is severely damaged, there's a significant probability that the capsule will burn up, killing the three crew members on board. The leader of the space mission at Houston's control center overhears a tense discussion between two of his mission leaders, one of whom whispers, "I know the problems. It will be the worst disaster NASA has ever experienced." The leader interrupts the gentlemen's discussion and boldly claims, "In all due respect, I believe this will be our finest hour."[1]

It's easy to fall prey to negative thinking in the midst of crisis. Panic takes precedence over perseverance, and thoughts of disaster take precedence over our determination to overcome.

We pray that whenever you hear that negative voice of doubt creep into your thoughts, you'll think confidently that this moment will be your finest hour.

Discussion Guide

- What are the most important things going on in your life right now? Prioritize them in order of importance.

- Where do you get your energy? List your energy-giving activities.

- What drains your energy? List your energy-draining activities.

- Identify your goals for the next year (SMART goals).

- What skill set and core competencies do you need to gain to be where you want to be in five years?

- What character and leadership development do you need?

Bold Choice 2:

Accountability

Taking Responsibility
for Your Life Journey

Fear of failure was found

to be the single largest contributor

to risk aversion and lack of

accountability in the workplace.

9

Accountability: From Fear of Failure to Embracing Failure

(Larry)

I distinctly remember my first owners' meeting as the sales and marketing director of a large hotel in Atlanta. I was in my early thirties, and this was my first significant leadership position. While I'd been recently promoted for being a good sales producer, I knew nothing about leadership. I wanted to make a good impression at this meeting but instead walked away with an indelible impression that accountability meant "produce or else."

The incredibly tense meeting included our executive team, members of our corporate office, and the owners of the hotel, who were angry and upset because the hotel was significantly off revenue projections.

There was one legitimate reason for the revenue decline—the increase in competition—but I recognized that the hotel and corporate office were also at fault. We didn't have a healthy culture of accountability but one of politics with every department looking out for its own interests. Quite frankly, I contributed to that lack of accountability, as I was more concerned about keeping my job than being a leader and helping my staff grow and achieve their goals.

During this difficult meeting, one of the owners took me aside and proceeded to read me the riot act. The guy stood an imposing six feet four inches tall, wore a tailored suit, and spoke with a thick Southern drawl similar to that of cartoon character Foghorn Leghorn. All I now remember was him saying, "If you don't produce by the fourth quarter, I will be all over you like white on rice!" That experience magnified my negative definition of accountability.

The months that followed produced a fear of failure that permeated from the top down. The message was very clear: "Failure is not an option." Our corporate office put pressure on the general manager, who put pressure on me, and I in turn put pressure on my sales staff. As the weeks progressed, our sales team broke down to "every man for himself" as everyone focused on saving their own job rather than learning and growing from our situation. Instead of being sailors courageously steering our ship into the winds of adversity, we were more like rats scattering to escape a sinking ship. Six months later I was fired, and I realized that it's tough to move forward with accountability when you're backpedaling in fear.

It's been thirty years since those challenging days. Today, as a leadership coach, I know that I was not alone regarding my fear of failure.

"Accountability is motivational

and an essential component of

our personal growth as leaders."

I've seen fear of failure and lack of accountability across the board: from entry-level employees to the CEO. These observations were confirmed for me in a September 5, 2013, American Management Association article where Jennifer Jones stated, "Fear of failure or making a mistake often causes employees to avoid taking responsibility for their actions, according to a survey by AMA Enterprises, a division of American Management Association International. This anxiety was found to be the single largest contributor to risk aversion and lack of accountability in the workplace. In the survey of executives, managers, and employees of more than 500 companies who participated 38% cited fear of being held responsible for mistakes or failures as the biggest obstacle."[1]

Accountability in business has been a front-and-center topic for decades. It's an important yet complex issue that includes many moving parts beyond fear of failure. Organizations face a myriad of intertwined causes, including competition between departments, poor communication, lack of buy-in, conflict and problem avoidance, and poor follow-through.

One of the hidden benefits of being an author is the privilege of writing stories about leaders I admire. I also write about topics I struggle with, and accountability is one of them. While I've come a long way since my hotel management days, I still deal with fear of failure. I can blame, avoid, and deflect my way out of personal accountability with the best of them.

I believe you will find Jay's insights on accountability refreshing, inspiring, and perhaps even convicting. I know that's what I experienced as I learned more of his story. He took a complex issue and simplified it so it makes sense. He also makes some bold claims that go against the grain of conventional business wisdom: "Accountability is motivational and an essential component of our personal growth as leaders. Success is to be celebrated. Failure is to be embraced." All of these endeavors lead us on our journey to fulfilling our potential.

Accountability goes way beyond business, and we need each other on this journey through life—not just from a motivational perspective but also for our protection.

10

Accountability Is Motivational

(Jay)

Most people don't want to be held accountable because they view it as a negative. Whether it's a boss's review or a to-do list on Saturday morning, the responsibility involved is unwelcome. For me, however, accountability is all about motivation. As tragic as my accident was, it gave me a second chance at life. My newfound faith provided so many blessings, one of which was accountability. Simply put, I discovered a deep sense of responsibility for others, particularly my family.

An example of this deep sense of accountability came in the hospital shortly after my accident. My wife, Jule, told me that our ten-year-old daughter, Alexa, would be coming in soon to see me. I immediately asked, "What do I look like?" and requested a mirror from the nurse. Grabbing it, I took a look at myself for the first time. "No way!" I shouted. "You've got to clean me up! I look terrible!" My skin looked like death—a yellowish gray—and my hair was a mess. The nurse cleaned me up the best she could, but I was still hooked up to a bunch of lines so I couldn't get out of bed and change into nice clothes.

The news that Alexa was coming to see me became a defining moment of accountability; it motivated me. I thought, *Man, I've got to start kicking this thing into gear!*

Alexa's visit was the first of a series of hurdles I was motivated to jump over. I went through extensive physical therapy and had to prove I could do the most basic things—get out of a wheelchair, get into a car, and perform a long list of menial tasks that I'd taken for granted my whole life—before I could be released from the hospital. In spite of the difficulty, I was accountable to my family and motivated to get back home.

I thanked God for this newfound sense of accountability because the toughest part of my journey began after I got out of the hospital. The hurdles I had to jump to be released paled in comparison to the ones yet to come: battling a four-year prison conviction, rebuilding my family life, keeping my job, and integrating prison life into my work and family life. My personal accountability motivated me to embrace these arduous challenges head-on.

Since then, I've discovered how essential accountability is. One of the biggest issues facing men is lack of accountability. When I ask them if they have anyone who holds them accountable, the answer I receive is usually no. Most men embrace a Lone Ranger attitude that insists they never expose their soft underbelly. They don't want to be vulnerable to attack, so they won't ask for help. They feel compelled to handle everything alone but can't. Instead, they say, "I got this," or "I can handle it."

The typical conversation between two guys goes something like this:

Bob: How you doing?

Fred: Good. How you doing?

Bob: Good.

Fred: How 'bout them Bears?

Now that we've established that both Bob and Fred are lying, now what? They can talk for hours about the Minnesota Vikings or Chicago Bears and never touch on what's really going on in their lives. But accountability is much more than friends asking, "How you doing?"

I'm chairman of Minnesota Adult and Teen Challenge, an organization that helps teens and adults overcome addiction, and we have over five hundred people in our program trying to beat addictions like alcohol, methamphetamine, and heroin. When they come out of our thirteen-month program, they need a community, because if they don't have accountability, they'll go right back to drugs.

Accountability has different levels. A small level of accountability would be something like reviewing business goals once a quarter to see how you're doing. Midlevel accountability would be meeting with your boss. A large level of accountability would be coming out of Minnesota Adult and Teen Challenge and having a community of people to hold you accountable so you don't end up going back to friends in the old neighborhood. While it's logical to apply more emphasis to the bigger levels of accountability, don't forget the importance of being accountable for the minor things. Small levels of accountability make a big difference. Are you present for your kids? Do you say, "I love you"?

We all need personal accountability in every aspect of life, not just in business. Accountability goes way beyond business, and we need each other on this journey through life—not just from a motivational perspective but also for our protection. I've found that most men live in isolation. We're on a journey, but we shouldn't travel by ourselves. There is great danger in being alone. Sometimes when we are alone, our thoughts and urges betray us and we make poor decisions.

Having a group of peers who know, love, and support you can make a huge difference in your life. Part of this support requires asking the hard questions. Being transparent isn't easy, but it's worth the effort. I highly recommend you join or create a small accountability group that will provide a safe environment that allows you to be transparent with others. It will help you grow as an authentic leader and be essential in your being accountable in your professional and personal life. Whether it's at work or home, embrace your accountability as a blessing that benefits you and others on your journey.

Achievement and Failure as Key Components of Accountability

Achievement

When you achieve something, do you celebrate or do you just move on to the next activity? Most people move on to the next activity, too busy to hold themselves accountable to learn, grow, and expand on what they're doing right. If we're going to persevere, we have to have some fun along the way. When we achieve something, we need to pause and celebrate. Achievement is a great learning tool. We need to ask ourselves what we did right, because we might want to repeat it. Remember, we're running a marathon, not a sprint. Enjoy the journey!

By taking the time to acknowledge we've done something right, we reinforce the right behavior. Pausing to celebrate our achievements is not just a learning tool; it's an important energy-giving strategy to replenish us in the midst of energy-sucking times. Most people believe they don't deserve to celebrate, so they just move to the next thing. This is a mistake. Sometimes it's the smallest acts that are worth recognizing and reinforcing.

As an example, my daughter, Alexa, was graduating medical school in Washington, DC, and needed help bringing her belongings back to Minnesota. I took time out of a busy schedule to fly out to Washington, DC, then drive back to Minnesota. I literally flew into Reagan National Airport, was picked up by my daughter, and started driving to Minneapolis. While this could have been viewed as a time-consuming chore, I saw it as a joyful, energy-producing experience with my daughter. I enjoyed the journey. While most would not categorize this as an achievement, I viewed it as such because it was a relationship-building experience.

While I didn't get a plaque with "Best Dad" engraved on it, I felt good. Our time together reinforced the intangibles of being a good father, so this small act was a behavior worth noting and reinforcing in the midst of my busyness. There are times when life is a grind and building in the smallest of celebrations can make a real difference.

Failure

The flipside of achievement is failure. A great quote from F. Scott Fitzgerald is, "Never confuse a single defeat with a final defeat."[1] Failure is the one of the things people think about when I use the word accountability. I don't know anyone who's had secular success but hasn't faced a lot of failure. I've failed a lot. While with Lawson Software, there was a time when I missed Wall Street's expectations, and it resulted in a $300

Bottom line,

when we're not accountable,

we're not demonstrating leadership.

million reduction in market cap in one day! Try to beat that. Investors screamed at me for two days.

Later I worked for XRS, a publicly traded company. Two times companies came in and tried to buy us. This meant bringing a bunch of people in and getting the executive team heavily involved. Both times the sale fell through because the price didn't meet investor expectations. It was too low; neither firm could come up with enough money to buy our company. Each time was considered a huge failure for our executive team, and as a result, they felt deflated and went into a funk. Their energy dropped way down. At the same time, the investors became anxious. These times felt like huge failures.

Most of the successful executives I know fail more than most. I certainly fail more than most people. In fact, I live by the popular adage, "If you're not failing, you're not trying." Oftentimes, I can make a decision, implement that decision, adjust my decision depending on whether it's right or wrong, and make another decision before most people make their first decision.

I've found that the higher I go, the less information will be black and white. Most businesses today require fast decisions because market conditions move so quickly. The technology industry was moving at light speed, so I needed to move just as fast, even when it came to making decisions in gray areas. Although many of my decisions weren't the right ones, I learned a great deal through each failure.

Anytime I failed, whether it was a small failure or a big one, whether it was by myself or with my team, I would do a debriefing consisting of three questions:

1. *What did I (or we) do right?* In this situation, most people start off by asking what they did wrong. This question puts many

on the defensive. Anyway, in most cases you're doing something right. Start with "What did I (we) do right?" because it helps change your paradigm, which helps you build on what's presently working.

2. *In hindsight, what would I (or we) have done differently?* This question increases your prudence in decision making. Now that you have more information, question how you would apply this wisdom for a better outcome the next time. This valuable process will help you improve and grow from mistakes.

3. *What am I (or we) going to change?* You might have seven things you would do differently but have the ability to change only one or two of them in the next month. Stay focused on the most important changes you need to make and then come back and do this debriefing exercise another month. Asking this question helps you better adapt to necessary change.

If we're going to persevere, we need to learn how to embrace failure, not fear it. I don't know anyone who's gone from point A to point B and hasn't experienced a few misfires. The key is to be accountable. As a CEO, I learned that the easiest way to spot poor leadership is to look at others' accountability for their area or people. I don't tolerate blame, excuses, or finger-pointing. People don't follow leaders who throw their people under the bus. Bottom line, when we're not accountable, we're not demonstrating leadership. And it's not so much about lack of accountability; rather, it's about stepping up as a leader and taking responsibility for our area. I strongly urge you to use debriefing as an effective accountability tool to move you forward in business and in life.

Concluding Thoughts on Accountability

Accountability is an integral part of leadership in every facet of our life at work and at home. As a business leader, I'm responsible for assessing risk and making wise decisions with others. I need to include whomever I'm involved with, including those who hold me accountable. Since failure is part of the game, I would go into a board meeting with confidence and not fear.

When I missed the mark and had to go in front of the board, I knew they didn't want to hear, "I don't know what the heck is going on." So I would boldly state, "Here's what we did right," "Here's what we learned," "Here's what we're going to do differently," and "Here are the changes we're going to make." This honest, straightforward approach creates positive accountability toward problem solving that helps all parties move forward. I have learned to have a small rearview mirror and a giant windshield. I spend zero time on the negative and apply all my time to the positive of moving forward.

As a leader in my personal life, accountability motivates me because it commits me to the personal goals I set for myself. It also strengthens my commitment to my family and others. I have a group of guys who hold me accountable because I know I can't do it alone. I lean on these men when I'm in need, and I'm there for them when they're in need.

Whether at work or at home, we are accountable. When we accept failure as part of the game, we accept responsibility to effectively learn and grow from it. When we achieve our goals, we should celebrate. When we understand that our actions go beyond ourselves and impact others on the journey, we recognize how important accountability is. We don't take this journey alone; we need each other. Accountability is the engine that keeps us on track to fulfill our potential.

11

Accountability Is an Asset, Not a Liability

(Larry)

Jay's redefinition of accountability was a huge paradigm shift for me. It inspired and convicted me, and through it I learned two powerful lessons:

1. *Accountability is born of deep responsibility for others, particularly family.* I was moved by Jay's motivation in the hospital to get cleaned up for the sake of his daughter. I found it heartwarming to see how seeds of personal responsibility can bloom out of tragic personal failure. His story certainly confirms F. Scott Fitzgerald's quote: "Never confuse a single defeat with a final defeat." Jay could have easily become the victim of his tragic accident, making it his final defeat. Instead, small seeds of accountability grew into a journey to

finding and fulfilling his potential. His personal accountability didn't allow the accident to define him; rather, it propelled him to become a better leader at work, at home, and in his community.

2. *Accountability is an asset, not a liability.* I was convicted by Jay's first statement: "When I say accountability, most people think negative because they don't want to be held accountable." As I shared in the introduction, I started my business career viewing accountability as a negative. For me, failure meant getting fired, and as a result, I've shied away from being accountable.

As I look back at my situation thirty years ago, I wonder if the outcome of the owners' meeting would have been different if I'd boldly ascribed to the type of accountability Jay defined. What if I had gone into that meeting prepared with "Here's what we are doing right," "Here's what we learned," and "Here are the changes we're going to make"? What if I'd felt a deep responsibility for my sales team instead of for saving my own skin? What if I'd had an accountability group to help me through my fears? Would it have changed the outcome?

We'll never know, but I do know this: it definitely would have changed me as a person and as a leader. I can't say whether I would have changed the outcome, but I believe my personal accountability would have had a significant impact on the people around me. Being personally accountable moves us and others forward in a positive and powerful way.

True success on any scale

requires each of us to not only accept

accountability but also embrace it as

a responsibility worthy of others' trust.

12

Accountability Is an Essential Part of the Journey

(Larry)

Perhaps the most insightful comment Jay made is the fact that accountability is an integral part of our journey. Accountability is indeed a motivation. True success on any scale requires each of us to not only accept accountability but also embrace it as a responsibility worthy of others' trust.

As Jay asserts, accountability is a journey that grows with maturity. It starts with how we personally define it, and it means being responsible for the things that are within our power and care. Putting this definition into action produces trustworthiness. In today's world where trustworthiness is a scarce commodity, trust is as precious as gold in your business and personal lives.

Accountability also produces prudence. A leader with sound judgment has high value in today's rapidly changing, volatile, and uncertain marketplace. Finally, accountability produces leaders, like Jay, who understand that they are answerable. They willingly take responsibility by giving an account for their actions in a bold, proactive way. They don't backpedal in fear but move forward and bring others along on the journey.

I'm a huge Minnesota Vikings fan. During the week I'm a relatively normal person, but come football season I head to my man cave on Sunday afternoon and transform into a raging maniac who shouts with joy and grunts in disgust. It allows me to blow off the steam of my week and argue with the refs on my television. *ABC's Wide World of Sports* captured this fanatical behavior when they coined the perfect phrase: "the thrill of victory and the agony of defeat."[1]

I was placed in that very moment of truth on Sunday, January 10, 2016, at 3:07 p.m. CST (but hey, who's keeping track?). This was the moment that Blair Walsh, kicker for the Minnesota Vikings, lined up for an easy twenty-seven-yard field goal that could win the NFL Wild Card playoff game against the Seattle Seahawks. With seconds remaining in the game, the Vikings valiantly marched down the field to set up, and Walsh lined up for a field goal that was considered a chip shot that kickers make 99 percent of the time. If he kicked it through the uprights, we won, and if he missed, we lost. Talk about pressure!

Amid the wild screams of sixty thousand fans, the ball was snapped and the kick was … wide to the left. He missed! The frenzy of screams fell to dead silence. Within a few minutes, Walsh was surrounded by a large crowd of reporters who barked questions at him like a group of frenzied seals. Bright lights blinded him, and cameras flashed to capture every twitch and contortion of a man on trial. Microphones were shoved close to his mouth to catch every groan, sigh, and comment on his epic failure now instantly spread worldwide. Within seconds, social media was torching this man in the cruelest ways possible.

In the center of this maelstrom stood Walsh, demonstrating the class and dignity of a standup guy who is accountable. He patiently repeated his full accountability for the missed field goal and answered for his mistake repeatedly with each reporter's question. In this situation, he could have made some legitimate excuses for missing the ball—it was two degrees below zero, the snap was high, or the holder didn't position the ball laces out. Instead, Walsh took full responsibility.

This incident reminded me of my childhood. I'd always loved baseball, and growing up in New York, I was a big Yankees fan. Back in the 1960s, the Yankees played in the World Series on several occasions. Each fall during the World Series, the *New York Daily News* posted a segment titled "Heroes and Goats." After each game the paper would identify the hero from the winning team and the goat from the losing team (someone who made an error contributing to the loss of his team). Typically, a caricature of the hero was created in a positive light and the goat was created with a sad face and goat horns. Looking back, while I admit that it was humorous and fun to read, I also see that it planted seeds into millions of kids that failure is bad and those who fail are punished and mocked.

While the ridicule for Blair Walsh continued for days, there were also supporters who demonstrated kindness, compassion, and mercy. I especially appreciated the first grade class in Minneapolis that sent Walsh letters of encouragement and support on the Monday that followed. This wise teacher seized the opportunity to teach empathy to young children who were indirectly exposed to the public display of ridicule of a man who was attempting to do his best but failed in the clutch. Walsh was so moved by the empathy of these students that he visited

Looking at the big picture,
accountability has a positive impact
in every facet of your life—spiritual,
personal, and professional.

the class to say thank you. His comments to the class spoke volumes. As he had before, he made no excuses: "I take accountability and owner-ship. And that's a big lesson for you."[2] Throughout his visit, he expressed thanks to the students for their kindness and encouraged them to always do their best.

There's a great lesson about accountability to be gleaned from Blair Walsh. He did his best, failed, owned it, learned from it, and moved on. Clearly, in sports, business, and life, failure plays a role. As Jay shared, failure is part of the game. Don't confuse one defeat with a final defeat.

What inspires me most about Jay and Blair Walsh is their focus on the journey and not the outcome. Both leaders didn't let a failure define them. They took full responsibility and moved forward with dogged determination to continue on the journey and realize their full potential.

Both stories are extreme, but I believe the same principle applies to your life and leadership. The smallest acts of accountability can make a huge difference in your life, and you impact countless lives because you take your responsibility seriously. Looking at the big picture, accountability has a positive impact in every facet of your life—spiritual, personal, and professional.

This is obvious from a spiritual point of view. The parable of the talents provides a powerful message that you are accountable for the gifts and talents God has given you. Burying your talents out of fear is a waste of your life, but being accountable for them brings great joy to God and others around you. Jay once stated, "No one is good at every-thing, but we are good at some things." This is reflected in the parable of the talents: "His master replied, 'Well done, good and faithful servant! You have been faithful with a few things; I will put you in charge of many things. Come and share your master's happiness!'" (Matthew 25:21).

When you're faithful, you're being responsible with what has been placed in your care. You are reliable and worthy of others trust. Whether to your boss, your family, or your friends, your accountability brings joy to God and positively influences others. In essence, when you grow and mature as an accountable leader, it has a significant positive impact on the people around you. Be accountable for your life. It's the only one you have. This is a noble pursuit that is inspiring and motivating!

Discussion Guide

- When you achieve a particular goal, do you celebrate or just move on to the next goal? Explain.

- How do you receive failure? Do you receive it in a positive light and learn from it, or do you view it as a negative and stew on it?

- How do you view accountability? Is it motivational for you or is it something you avoid?

- What's your biggest lesson learned from this chapter on accountability?

Bold Choice 3:

Adaptability

Personal Change

Precedes Practical Change

Sometimes pain and discomfort

can be good things, serving as

a built-in alarm clock that warns

us about complacency

and awakens us to action.

13

Death by Denial: Settling for Comfortably Numb

(Larry)

The dream is gone.
I've become comfortably numb.[1]
—Pink Floyd

Change and the importance of adaptability have been front-and-center topics in business leadership for as long as I can remember. Many good speakers talk about viable solutions that range from resilience, creativity, and organizational learning, to dealing with stress. These strategies, though great, often fail because they rarely address the core issue: change can be painful. For that reason, people resist in a variety of ways, such as through denial, avoidance, or simply becoming comfortably numb.

I've kept in touch with several college buddies through the years, and it deeply saddens me that some have settled into a life that is comfortably numb. One friend was an extremely talented and passionate leader who was downsized by his company, and he settled for a lesser job just for a paycheck. He needs to work but hates his job. And while he accepts this reality, he has lost his passion. Another friend built a successful business out of his passion for engineering. When technology changed his field of work, he sold his company and retired. He lives comfortably on his retirement, playing golf as much as possible, but he's bored with life.

This issue doesn't affect just baby boomers. I've seen many bright, young emerging leaders let a series of painful personal and professional failures derail them from fulfilling their potential because they're afraid to embrace the tougher right road.

Bottom line, change can be painful. Sometimes it's abrupt like Jay's accident. Other times it's a slow, foreseeable process, but we delay or avoid doing something about it because we prefer not to deal with the discomfort associated with the change. In some ways, I think slow change is harder to deal with because it doesn't demand immediate action; it is also more dangerous because we can become comfortably numb. Sometimes pain and discomfort can be good things, serving as a built-in alarm clock that warns us about complacency and awakens us to action.

Regardless of your particular situation, I hope Jay's story awakens you to embrace and adapt to change as an important step in your journey to realizing your potential.

Your Worst Nightmare Is Here! Deal with It!

Imagine sitting in your wheelchair slowly recovering from a horrific accident with a shattered hip and a shattered heart after losing your dad and best friend. You then open a letter from the state and are staring at the words *four-year prison sentence*. This moment was the beginning of a living-nightmare boxing match that had Jay fighting for his life. The rounds included his preparing for a trial, keeping his job, going to jail, and then balancing jail time with family and work.

Throughout this time, he learned an invaluable lesson in adaptability. He learned that change, no matter how painful, must be confronted head-on. His two most valuable essentials were continuous learning and adaptability. The more he practiced them, the more he grew from change. When I asked Jay how he went from convicted felon to CEO, he told me that the same essentials of continuous learning and adaptability that got him through his nightmare also laid the groundwork for becoming a successful CEO.

Let's learn from Jay how he used these tools to transform his life.

If I looked at all the obstacles stacked

on top of each other, they would

have been too overwhelming

to overcome, so I adapted by

chunking them and focusing on

solving one problem at a time.

14

Convict to CEO

(Jay)

To quote Leon C. Megginson, "It's not the strongest of the species that survives, nor the most intelligent, but the one most responsive to change."[1] As I look back on my life, I certainly wasn't the strongest or the most intelligent, but I was adaptable to change. Few of my plans have allowed me to go from point A to point B without my making some kind of dramatic change. In each situation, I had to adapt. My first revelation about the power of adaptability came shortly after I graduated from high school.

My high school academic career in Philadelphia was pretty lame. I was getting Ds and Fs and had to scramble to make sure I didn't have to go to summer school. After graduation, I wound up working in construction. I then dislocated my shoulder playing rugby and dislocated it another five times due to my lifestyle. I couldn't work, so I ended up going to a community college to fill my time.

A fortunate turn of events came about in college: the one marketing course I took had a great teacher. I actually applied myself, and the business world came alive for me. When I would drive home from school, I could see it in action. I could see advertising. I could see promotion. I could see distribution.

All of a sudden, I couldn't get enough of education and information. I developed the insatiable appetite for knowledge of the business world that I still have to this day. This continuous learning helped me adapt to change in business and in life.

By far, my biggest life-altering event was my accident. It set in motion a series of events that revealed why adapting to life's circumstances is so important. I hope this journey that began with my accident on January 3, 1998, and culminated with successfully taking Lawson Software public on December 7, 2001, can give you a better understanding of why adapting to change is an essential part of your personal and professional life.

Fighting for My Life

I was in my wheelchair out on the driveway when I received the letter from the state of Minnesota. Two things I read struck fear into my heart: *We're prosecuting you for criminal vehicular homicide*, and *four-year prison sentence*.

In a panic, my wife and I threw the wheelchair into our truck and drove around to see a bunch of lawyers. They all said basically the same thing: "Jay, if we do everything right and all the stars line up, you won't have to do four years in prison. You'll only have to do two years. That's if everything goes perfectly."

I answered with a question each time: "What's plan B? Because that ruins my life." It meant going through an eight-month trial (and, by the way, I was guilty!). What a frightening reality considering that two years in prison appeared to be the best possible sentence for criminal vehicular homicide.

At this point, a lot of people were trying to help, saying things like, "Oh, you don't have to worry about going to jail because it's your dad," or "Don't worry about it. You'll get out of it." Their hearts were in the right place, but their hope was idealistic. I needed realistic hope.

I found a good lawyer named Bill. The months leading up to the trial became a life of two worlds—and a roller coaster of highs and lows. In the morning, I would go to work at Lawson Software, where my division was doing great. It was good to see my team do well, but I couldn't bring in the horrors of my trial into the workplace when everyone was so fired up. Then, at the end of the day, the team would often ask me to join them after work to celebrate our many victories. I came up with excuses because I had to go back to the stressful reality of meeting my lawyer. I felt like I was leading a double life.

From late afternoon until early evening, I would meet with Bill. I was getting educated on what it really meant to commit a felony, and continuous learning and adaptability became a huge asset. I pored over information on the judicial system and the process that determined jail time. (Learning about sentencing guidelines was critical because it showed me what level my crime was and how much time I would serve.) As painful as this was, it helped me strategize my options and develop a game plan to get the shortest possible jail time.

Although I disliked spending so much time doing this, I was collecting data that would help me make the best decision of the worst choices available to me. Each day I learned how the judicial system works and adapted to an environment completely foreign to me. I came to the realization that jail time was inevitable and said to Bill, "The most jail time I can do and keep my job is six months." He told me that would be a stretch, but he would do his best.

I'll never forget the day of the trial when Bill came out of the judge's chambers and said, "I got the judge to agree to six months and ten years' probation." I stepped close and asked, "Is this the best I'm going to get?" When he replied, "Jay, you'd be stupid not to take it," I immediately agreed to it. I certainly didn't want to go to jail, but the sentence would achieve my ultimate goal of keeping my job and moving on with life. I learned to adapt to a bad situation by getting the best outcome I could get. I was going to prison but was determined get through it and rebuild my life.

The Roller-Coaster Ride Continues

In the days leading up to my prison term, Lawson put on a big event in New Orleans. My division had performed incredibly well for the year, and I was heading to New Orleans to celebrate our success, all the while dreading my prison sentence.

My time at the event was surreal. I was about to address an audience of three hundred Lawson employees at our meeting, the first time most people in the audience were seeing me since my accident. I was walking with a cane and slowly made my way up to the stage. When I approached the microphone to make my presentation, I received a standing ovation from my peers—one of the highlights of my business career! What a poignant moment as I thought, *Standing ovation, going to jail.*

As I flew back to Minneapolis, the high point of my standing ovation in New Orleans was replaced by the sickening roller-coaster drop into the stark reality of jail time. Once again, I would need to adapt and try to hold my life together. There were times when I tired of battling one problem after another. If I looked at all the obstacles stacked on top of each other, they would have been too overwhelming to overcome, so I adapted by chunking them and focusing on solving one problem at a time.

First, I tried to figure out how to be a dad to my three kids—two young sons and a daughter—while in jail. I didn't want them coming to jail and seeing me in an orange jumpsuit. That wasn't going to be a picture they'd ever have of me. So I figured out how my boys could see me in a seminormal setting—by having Jule bring them to my work during my lunch hour while I was in the work release program.

I was confined to my workplace, so I needed to find a place to have lunch and play with the boys. Lawson had a small hole-in-the-wall gym in the basement, which worked well, but I wasn't able to see my daughter because she was in school during the day. Again, I created a plan. I bought her a gigantic teddy bear and explained that it was going to have to replace her daddy for a while. I practiced that speech more than I've ever practiced any speech in my life. And I'm happy to say that my daughter, who is now twenty-six and just graduated med school, still has the teddy bear. That's a big deal for me.

I also couldn't drive, so I had to figure a way to get to and from jail. My wife couldn't drive me because she was taking care of our three kids, so I had to find friends who could take me to and from jail. Relying on them was a good learning experience for me as I realized that I didn't have to go through my ordeal alone.

Finally, I had to adapt to life in jail. I'll be honest. It really sucked. When I first met other prisoners, they would say, "Where you from?"

and I'd answer, "Eden Prairie, Minnesota." But what they really were asking was what other prison system I had come from and what I was in for. It didn't take me long to realize I was in a foreign environment that required quick adaptation and fast adjustment. What a humbling experience. I lost my freedom. I had guards telling me what to do, and I went through the humiliation of being strip-searched. Prison life was certainly an adjustment. Adapting was not a choice but a necessity.

I learned a lot in prison, like how big a deal it was to lose my freedom. Jail time helped me put things in the proper perspective, and I recognized the importance of clarity to discover what's really important. It also heightened my sense of accountability to others, particularly my family. I had to adapt in order to survive. Ultimately, I was motivated to not be defined by this difficult time in my life. I had a family to look after, a career to reestablish, and a God-given potential to realize. I was determined to persevere and overcome every barrier in my way.

Convict to CEO

Even though I wore a house arrest ankle bracelet, I was growing in my role as the executive vice president of sales and service. A lot of change was taking place at Lawson, as the small software company I'd joined years before had gone from $10 million in revenue to about $150 million. We were one of the last companies not to go public, but Lawson was finally considering it. Soon, large investment banking companies like Goldman Sachs and J. P. Morgan were visiting our company.

The owners, Bill and Richard Lawson, were developers, so they were new to the process of going public. Bill always invited me to go with him to meet potential investors, and beforehand we would create a slide presentation. Bill would do the first slide and then hand it over to me so I could conduct the rest of the presentation. We did this for about a year, and every time I presented to the bankers, someone would say something like, "Jay, great job, wrong job title. You're not the one who can take it public. You need to be CEO."

Bill was the CEO, but I wasn't pushing for his role because he had done everything for me. I was just doing the work that needed to be done, and in the process I learned every aspect of the process of going public. I was learning from the investment bankers, and we were changing the company's strategy, hiring new people and redesigning a new board. Bill eventually said, "Well, you've got to be CEO."

As I took over as CEO of Lawson Software, we focused on going public in the fall of 2001. Incredible amounts of planning and preparation took place through the summer months. The board was eager, the employees were excited, and so many activities lead to a rousing crescendo.

Then 9/11 happened. In one tragic day, years' worth of work ended in an instant. Everything was put on hold. I knew we had to adapt and adjust quickly, keeping the team focused and motivated in spite of the unfortunate turn of events. I'm proud to say that while we were all discouraged, we kept our focus and never complained or lost hope. The team remained motivated and positive. When the investors came back to us in November, we were ready to go. We hit the ground running in New York with our roadshow, and on December 7, 2001, we went public, becoming the fifth-largest IPO in Minnesota history.

The Bottom Line

On January 3, 1998, I had an accident that changed my life forever. I took an improbable trek from convicted felon to CEO of one of the largest public companies in Minnesota. But as painful as that four-year journey was, learning to adapt to change helped me grow in ways I never thought possible.

Life has certainly normalized since those turbulent times, but even with a "normal" life, I'm constantly confronted with changes in my professional and personal realms. Looking back now, I see that my ability to adapt to change has become an inherent core trait that has served me well though the years.

On a personal front, I had to adapt to the many physical limitations of my body. I could no longer run for exercise because of my various pins, plates, and scars, so I took up biking and still bike to this day. I used to love playing basketball with my sons and wanted to somehow continue this connection to my boys, so I've gone through various alternative medical treatments and exercises to rebuild my health. I may not play like Michael Jordon, but I can play basketball with my kids.

On a professional front, adaptability was a key to my success as a CEO. After my time at Lawson Software, I became the CEO of XRS Corporation, based in Eden Prairie, Minnesota. We grew our company revenues from $20 million to $50 million, but our strategy needed to change to make a greater return on investment.

I could see the mobile revolution coming and started changing to a mobile app strategy. I bought a mobile application company at the end of 2009, and then the strategy was reinforced when Steve Jobs came out with a digital tablet in 2010. I again altered the company's strategy by switching to mobile devices for our fleet of trucks. It took us about three years, but we achieved our goal and ended up selling the company for more than $170 million.

Adapting to change and continuous learning are two critical elements that will help you persevere through life's roller coaster of ups and downs. In life you're either going forward or falling backward. If you're not adapting to the changes around you, you're going to either stall out or get stuck, and you'll eventually quit.

What kind of roller-coaster ride are you on? Life's going to take you up, and life's going to take you down. How are you going to get through it? How are you going to adapt?

Think back over the last five years. How much have you adapted professionally? How much have you adapted personally? Now think through the next five years. How will you adapt to the changes in your personal and professional lives? How will your business be relevant in a changing marketplace? How will you grow physically, emotionally, and spiritually? These are important questions worth pondering, because nothing remains the same. We must adapt.

In Ecclesiastes, Solomon states, "There is a time for everything, and a season for every activity under the heavens" (3:1). Life is certainly a roller coaster of highs and lows. Why not embrace the entire ride? Don't let your fears, biases, and skill sets stop you from adapting and growing in every season. Life is short. Adapt and enjoy the ride.

Personal faith and practical secular skills

are not intended to be contradictory

but complementary; they don't compete

with each other but are companions.

15

Transformed by Trials from the Inside Out

(Larry)

Everyone thinks of changing the world,
but no one thinks of changing himself.
—Leo Tolstoy[1]

I've been working in the area of integrating business leadership and faith for over twenty years. To this day, it's one of the most misunderstood areas in leadership development. Personal faith and practical secular skills are not intended to be contradictory but complementary; they don't compete with each other but are companions. Bottom line, personal change comes from the inside out. Personal transformation precedes practical application.

For me, 1994 to 2001 was a difficult seven years. I felt a strong calling to write a business leadership book on how to integrate faith and work, but I knew nothing about writing or publishing. In the following years, I learned every aspect of writing and publishing, and in terms of practical skills, I believed I'd become a pretty good writer. Even so, my skills and confidence didn't prepare me for what lay ahead. I had to pack up three years of dedicated work into a book proposal and then try to find a publisher.

This became a grueling road of close to forty rejections. I shopped the book to twenty literary agents before finding one who became my agent. We then went through nineteen rejections over the next three years. The final rejection was the straw that broke the camel's back, and I quit, angrily lashing out at God and blaming him for wasting my time.

Several weeks later, I came back to God with my tail between my legs and with a sense of peace and surrender. Even though it made no practical sense, I decided to just write what was on my heart and let go of the idea of ever getting the book published. For the next year I wrote the remainder of the book, which turned out to be my best work; the writing was more transparent and relevant to the reader.

Almost a year after that, we found a publisher to publish my first book, *God Is My CEO*. As I look back now, I realize that I had developed all the practical skills to write a book but not the maturity to be the author. Personal transformation preceded practical application. I needed to authentically become the author before having my words printed in a book, and my journey helped me serve others with a clear sense of purpose.

Today, I have the privilege of working with emerging leaders who have significant skills and core competencies to succeed in business. While these practical skills are essential, my primary focus is on developing their personal character. We all have been given unique gifts, and it's important to understand that developing our character enables us to practically apply these gifts.

There is no better training ground for character than the trials in life. It seems completely counterintuitive when the apostle James exclaims, "Blessed is the one who perseveres under trial " (James 1:12). We wonder, *How are we blessed by trials?* Tolstoy's quote provides a large part of the answer: we must first be changed before we can change the world.

If we look at Jay's journey from convict to CEO, we clearly see a man who has been blessed by persevering through his trials. He is a very different man today than he was on January 2, 1998, just twenty-four hours before his accident. With that in mind, let's take a closer look at how his personal transformation and practical skill application came into play while he adapted to the changes that took place between then and now.

Practical Peace and Realistic Hope

When you think of peace and hope, what comes to mind? A Hallmark card with soft, flowery images? Holding hands with your loved one while watching a sunset? We typically don't associate peace and hope with the blood, sweat, and tears of life that come with losing a loved one, trying to save a marriage, or overcoming a failure. I think these words are more like putting on boxing gloves in the ring of life—tools of the trade. They protect us from the blows of life and help us knock down the real-life obstacles that threaten. Specifically, let's look at how Jay used these tools to adapt to the challenges of his journey.

Practical Peace

As you may recall, Jay descended into a dark place the moment he received the letter from the state charging him with criminal vehicular homicide.

The prospect of serving a four-year jail sentence brought an awful sense of dread. With each passing day his anxiety grew with negative thoughts of losing his job, his house, and his wife and family. Worry kept him up in the middle of the night and carried over to his waking hours.

Perhaps the most practical action Jay took was to turn his worries over to God in prayer. Jay specifically found comfort in Philippians 4:6–9:

> Do not be anxious about anything, but in every situation, by prayer and petition, with thanksgiving, present your requests to God. And the peace of God, which transcends all understanding, will guard your hearts and your minds in Christ Jesus.
>
> Finally, brothers and sisters, whatever is true, whatever is noble, whatever is right, whatever is pure, whatever is lovely, whatever is admirable—if anything is excellent or praiseworthy—think about such things. Whatever you have learned or received or heard from me, or seen in me—put it into practice. And the God of peace will be with you.

Peace is not the absence of conflict and storms but the presence of calm within the storm. First, peace gave Jay the ability to overcome the negative self-talk that plagued him and provided the ability to think clearly in the midst of his storm. This peace of mind enabled him to endure long, stressful days balancing his job at Lawson Software, strategizing with his lawyer, and maintaining some sense of positive family life.

Second, peace enabled Jay to take action and confront every difficult task in front of him. One brilliant, practical strategy he employed was "chunking" his problems into doable actions. All the challenges stacked against him were too overwhelming as a whole, so he prioritized each obstacle into manageable actions. He found clarity in the chaos by taking on one problem at a time, one day at a time.

Realistic Hope

On a summer evening years ago, my wife and I camped with three other couples, each of whom had children under three years old. As evening turned to darkness, we observed a strong storm approaching in the distance. We initially thought we could handle it in our tents, but then the tornado sirens went off. We panicked, trying to come up with some action plan. One of the fathers said, "Let's pray" and proceeded to tell God that we placed our hope in him to protect us. He was coming from a place that said, *Let's do nothing and hope God will protect us.* Meanwhile, I was coming from a place that pleaded, *Let's take action and save ourselves.*

In reality, these two perspectives work together. Hope is not an *either/or* proposition but a *both/and* opportunity. We need to hope in the Lord for those things out of our control as well as do our part and take action.

I like Jay's concept of realistic hope. He shared that he had loved ones and friends who meant well in offering encouragement but were uneducated about the reality of the situation. In contrast, Jay had realistic hope, which allowed him to believe that "with God all things are possible" while also learning about and adapting to a rigid judicial system. Realistic hope became a positive and practical form of action in the midst of dire circumstances.

16

Change Yourself, Change Your Destiny

(Larry)

As Tolstoy's quote indicates, Jay needed to change himself before he could change his circumstances and future destiny. The change of his heart became what allowed him to adapt to the myriad of problematic situations that awaited him after he left the hospital. In Jay's case, personal transformation worked hand in glove with practical application. His change of heart enabled the work of his hands. The core blessings of peace and hope became the tools of his trade as he labored to rebuild his life.

How about you? What kind of roller-coaster ride are you on? As Jay boldly claims, "Life's going to take you up, and life's going to take you down. How are you going to get through it? How are you going to adapt?" I hope that Jay's story provides inspiration for your better tomorrow. As we mentioned, change can be painful but becoming comfortably numb is not the answer. Maybe the dreams you had have been altered or delayed, but they're not gone.

I remember a warm summer evening many years ago when my daughter Grace was six years old. She and I were gazing up at the night sky, and she declared, "There aren't any stars in the sky!" Because she couldn't see them behind the hazy clouds, she assumed they were gone.

There are times in life when things get a bit hazy. A better future lies ahead, but sometimes it's hidden behind the clouds of present circumstances. If you're feeling a bit stuck, I share this verse from the book of Jeremiah: "For I know the plans I have for you,' declares the Lord, 'plans to prosper you and not to harm you, plans to give you hope and a future'" (Jeremiah 29:11).

Discussion Guide

- Describe a time in your life when you needed to adapt. How did it change your life?

- Describe a period when your life seemed like a roller coaster. How did you adapt? What lessons learned did you take away from that experience?

- How do you find "practical peace" and "realistic hope" when you're in a difficult situation?

- What's your most important takeaway from this chapter?

Bold Choice 4:

Confidence

Keeping Your Thoughts
in Proper Perspective

Lack of confidence keeps us stuck because of fear, while overconfidence can lead to self-destruction because of pride. They both are barriers to realizing our potential.

17

The Battle Within

(Larry)

Imagine yourself in the Louvre Museum in Paris. You're sitting about twenty feet from the *Mona Lisa*, observing three young artists as they stop to view the classic masterpiece by Leonardo da Vinci.

The first artist walks up to the painting and whispers, "I could never create art like that," and walks off with his head hanging low. The second artist boasts, "My work is better than that!" and walks off without viewing the painting. The third artist, upon observing the painting, weeps in deep appreciation of its true value. He's humbled by its beauty and takes time to study its craftsmanship. Eventually, he walks away after telling you that he's been stirred to advance his craft so he too can inspire others through his art.

Each artist had a perspective, but only the third artist kept things in proper perspective. The first individual lacked confidence, while the second was overconfident. Their perspectives limited their potential.

However, the third was humble enough to put his response in the appropriate perspective. He wasn't intimidated by great work; he was inspired by it. He felt confident because his focus was not on himself but on the motivation to do excellent work in service to something greater than himself.

Confidence is essential on our journey to realizing our full potential. Jay defines confidence as keeping things in proper perspective—knowing the truth and being prepared. I think this definition is spot on. Perspective is our own particular outlook on the world. It's subjective, and it's what we see and believe regardless of whether it's true or not. Having the right perspective is critical.

Let me get to the heart of an issue we all face: Lack of confidence keeps us stuck because of fear, while overconfidence can lead to self-destruction because of pride. They both are barriers to realizing our potential. However, having the right perspective gives us the confidence to see what's true and prepare for what lies ahead. Allow me to use some of my own past perspectives as examples. My four-year stint of writing *God Is My CEO* created a wide array of emotions that significantly impacted my confidence level at various times in the journey.

The Bad, the Good, and the Ugly

The Bad

On a cold January morning in 1999, I was sitting in a coffeehouse trying to start my day. I got a second cup of high octane java in an attempt to get some semblance of inspiration but to no avail. I had just received my 17th publisher rejection letter, though it felt like my 187th. I had no inspiration to write, so I decided to go over to the local Borders bookstore. I regularly researched local bookstores' business section to check out new books. That morning, as I sat cross-legged on the floor at

Borders bookstore, I remember feeling totally insignificant and inadequate. I stared at the long row of leadership books. Feeling very sorry for myself, I started a negative self-talk dialogue that went something like this. "This is impossible! How in the world am I going to have my book sitting in bookstores with these leadership giants? I don't even deserve to be on the same shelf with them!"[1]

My lack of confidence wasn't doing me any favors. While it's legitimate and human to feel the sting of rejection, I compounded the issue by sentencing myself to a self-imposed jail of inaction. That was bad.

The Good

God Is My CEO finally got published and came into the world with a splash in the spring of 2001.

God Is My CEO just hit the bookstores. I had never written a book before so I had no idea what to expect. You can imagine how surprised I was when I received a phone call from the producer of *The 700 Club* television program. She inquired whether I would like to be interviewed by Pat Robertson, the program's founder. Knowing that this would be great publicity for my book, I quickly agreed to be on the show. The producer explained that she would finalize the dates and get back to me shortly to discuss the arrangements.

After hanging up, I leaped out of my chair in excitement! I ran upstairs to my wife, Sherri, and exclaimed, "Hey, guess what? I'm going to be on TV!" My only previous experience on television was the time I stood behind a reporter at a ball game and waved at the camera mouthing, "Hi Mom!"

About an hour later, the producer called me back to discuss final dates and details of the show. She said, "You'll have approximately eight minutes for the interview and of course, we'll want to hear your testimony." All of a sudden, I felt this overwhelming anxiety in the pit of my stomach. After I hung up, I quickly looked up *The 700 Club* website. My eyes fixed on the one sentence that blazed across the screen, *CBN reaches 160 million viewers in 127 countries.* The excitement of this huge opportunity quickly became a foreboding sense of dread!

Although I'm a speaker and have no problem standing in front of a group, the thought of being on television and baring my soul to the world was another matter. In the weeks leading up to the interview, I was plagued by an overwhelming fear. I felt stuck. I was committed to doing this but my brain saw the worst. I painted a picture of being on camera with millions watching and then just freezing in silence, stumbling over words and even throwing up while on the air. I know it was irrational, but I couldn't get this negative scene out of my head.

I arrived at CBN headquarters in Virginia on a spectacular spring evening to stay at their hotel before our interview the next morning. I practically had the entire grounds to myself as I walked along the beautiful grounds nestled among the pines. I tried to rehearse sound bite type "talking points" for my upcoming interview but still had considerable anxiety about the unknown of the next morning's interview.

As I walked around, I approached an area the size of a football field. Spaced equally apart were huge white satellite disks, each the size of a house, pointed in all directions. It was an awesome sight to behold! I started to think, "Wow, my testimony is going to be beamed across the world tomorrow morning." I stood in wonder of the awesome power of God and suddenly felt humbled and honored to play a small part in His plan. As I stood in awe, the anxiety drained from my body. I actually felt at peace![2]

When I shed my self-centered anxieties and got my ego out of the way, all that was left was the privilege of showing up and being the person God created me to be, warts and all. I felt liberated! The pressure to perform was gone. At that moment I was able to put things in proper perspective. I shed the negative self-talk and focused on the reality of the opportunity. This peace allowed me to calmly prepare for my interview.

The next morning the interview went fine. I was not perfect, showing some nerves associated with being on television, but I was authentic in sharing my testimony. I was humble and confident enough to share my views associated with writing *God Is My CEO*. Walking away from that interview, I had increased confidence in myself, not just for overcoming my fears but also for serving a greater good beyond myself. The act itself set a precedent for future opportunities. This was good.

The Ugly

Fast-forward two and a half years to the fall of 2003. *God Is My CEO* had become a best seller! I received great reviews in the *Wall Street Journal*, *CNN.com*, and *Inc.* magazine, as well as countless e-mails from people telling me how much the book impacted their lives. My ego was growing with each accolade, and I had to increase my hat size because my head was swelling!

I went to the same Borders bookstore I went to when I was a "nobody" trying to get published. This time I wasn't researching other leadership books but marveling at the prominent display of *God Is My CEO* on the bookshelf as if it was a monument to my own greatness. I walked over to the counter to ask for the store manager to see if we could order more books to make the awareness of *God Is My CEO* even more prominent, and I'll never forget the look on the store manager's face. (As they say, a picture is worth a thousand words.) His expression basically said, *What an arrogant jerk!*

Ouch! He was right. This was ugly.

Closing Thoughts

So, how in the world can one person have a lack of confidence, be confident, and then become arrogant and overconfident in the span of four years? The answer is simple: humans are susceptible to the ever-changing circumstances that can play tricks on the mind. That's why Jay's definition of *confidence* is so insightful. It's easy to lose focus, and we need to keep things in proper perspective.

When you have an honest, authentic, and humble sense of self, you have a powerful understanding of your capabilities. This humility, defined as "power under control," helps you develop the type of confidence that Jay describes in the following pages.

The biggest lesson I've learned

through accepting Jesus into my life

during my ordeal after the

accident was humility.

18

Redefining Confidence by Changing the Lens from Arrogance to Humility

(Jay)

When my youngest son, Tyler, was about five years old, he wanted to learn to ride a two-wheeled bike. Seeing his older brother and sister ride motivated him to shed his training wheels. He and I were in the driveway getting ready, and we talked over the routine of how I would run next to the bike to keep him from falling. I got the training wheels off his bike, and all of a sudden, he jumped on it and flew down our steep driveway, across the cul-de-sac, and toward a steep, winding path through the woods.

I jumped on my bike and peddled feverishly to catch up to him. Tyler looked over me and confidently shouted, "Watch and learn!" I yelled back, "That's interesting, Ty, because I haven't shown you how to hit the brakes and you've got a left turn coming up!" The next thing we knew, he was sprawled on the ground amid the dirt, leaves, and bushes. He didn't get hurt, but he learned an important lesson: being overconfident can cause you harm.

As saying goes, "The apple doesn't fall far from the tree." By nature I'm a confident person. But I've learned that I need to be aware of when my confidence becomes overconfidence—to keep things in proper perspective. All through my years in business, I've seen people suffer the consequences of either a lack of confidence or overconfidence. The former is dominated by fear and the latter by arrogance. Keeping things in proper perspective has been so important for me. It helps me keep myself in check when things are going well and provides encouragement when things aren't.

When I took our company public, I had a lot of people telling me how great I was. Well, guess what? I was not all that great. When I missed our quarterly goals, I had people telling me I was an idiot. I'm not an idiot either.

Personal Transformation Leads to Practical Application

Leadership development is a process that works from the inside out. Personal transformation leads to practical application. The biggest lesson I've learned through accepting Jesus into my life during my ordeal after the accident was humility. This fundamental shift had me questioning, "Who am I and what am I all about?" For me, humility became about caring for others, which was a huge change from life being about me to it being about others.

Before the accident I was as arrogant as the day is long. People didn't consider me a bad guy, but I was all about me and would crush anyone who got in my way. I worked in an industry that paid well and that meant winning in the marketplace. Truth be told, it was about me, myself, and I. Taking was much more important than giving.

As I look back now, from a business perspective, if I hadn't learned humility, I wouldn't be where I am today. I wouldn't have had employees who followed me, because people don't want to follow someone who's self-seeking. When my attitude shifted drastically, I wanted the people who worked for me to grow. Leadership development became essential, and I wanted each member of my leadership team to be a CEO someday. That shift resulted in a team of highly skilled, motivated, and dedicated leaders who wanted to succeed. I was more focused on wanting our organization to succeed than on my personal gain.

This change was what helped me define confidence as keeping things in proper perspective, because humility enabled me to not fear when things went bad and to not have my ego stroked when things went well. It was all about being prepared and knowing the truth.

Being Prepared

When we were going on the road to speak to potential buyers of Lawson Software, someone suggested that I get a speech coach to help me with my presentation. In my arrogance, I replied, "I don't need a speech coach. I do a lot of speaking, so I'm good." My investor friends insisted, so I finally relented and went to New York City to meet with a speech coach. She proceeded to tell me everything I needed to know about speaking. Then she said, "Jay, you need to memorize your speech." I quickly replied, "I don't memorize my speeches. I take a couple of bullets and just go with it." She asserted, "No. You're going to memorize your speech." After going back and forth, I eventually agreed.

She was absolutely right. I needed to memorize my speech. When doing a road show, people generally give their presentation between five and seven times a day. On one particular day in New York City, I gave the same presentation thirteen times. We started at 6:00 a.m. and ended at 9:00 p.m., and by the afternoon, I was getting a bit loopy. I couldn't remember if I'd told a particular joke, and things were getting confusing.

I would have never survived this day if I hadn't memorized my speech. I learned a big lesson about preparation. Being prepared gave me the confidence to do the job that was entrusted to me.

Knowing the Truth

Knowing the truth is the counter to negative self-talk. Do you remember my self-talk after receiving the news about potentially facing a four-year prison sentence? "I'm going to jail. If I go to jail, I'm going to lose my job. If I lose my job, I'm going to lose my house. If I lose my house, I going to lose my wife." It's so easy to let negative thoughts light a wildfire of panic in our minds, even when they're completely false.

We need to slow down, take some deep breaths, and get ourselves in the right frame of mind. As a friend once told me, "Get rid of the junk mail." (In reality, my wife wasn't leaving me. She was my greatest ally and supporter who was going to stick by me.) Don't make the situation worse. Slow down and take time to identify the truth.

We need the confidence to address the issue, whether it's major or minor. Sometimes people make a simple issue unnecessarily complex or undoable. If it's a minor issue, deal with it. If it's a major issue, break it down and figure out a solution. Most people, once the problem is broken down and simplified, relax and realize, *Okay, I can do this*. Knowing the truth helps us simplify and take action.

Whether the situation is personal or business related, knowing the truth provides the confidence to make the tough decisions and take action in the midst of challenging circumstances. When I was at XRS, I can't tell you how many people told me, "Don't do that mobile system. It's leading-edge technology that's too risky." I faced anger and pushback from customers and employees alike. But when I calmed myself down and studied the data, the research told me that going to mobile technology was the right thing to do.

Knowing the truth and being prepared gave me the confidence to make the hard decisions. Risk and uncertainty were real possibilities, but I felt confident because I'd done as much research as possible and had picked an alternative that I believed was right. I'd put in the necessary due diligence and effort to a make a wise, well-thought-out decision.

Once you've gone through all the data and facts that lead you to your tough choices, make the decision and move on. Finalize your plans and go with them. Skepticism and resistance to change will arise (and you may have to explain your decision fifty times over), but move forward and sell the plan with confidence.

Confident leaders have the humility to slow down and put things in proper perspective. They seek the truth and prepare for what lies ahead.

19

It's Not the Mountain We Conquer, but Ourselves

(Larry)

As an author and a leadership coach, I've been unofficially polling and researching businesspeople for over twenty-five years. In the vast majority, the issue of poor leadership comes down to either a lack of confidence or overconfidence on the leader's part. Both of these stem from the same root cause: too much focus on self.

Leaders who lack confidence often let their actions be dictated by their circumstances. They either see their situations as too difficult to conquer or they worry about what others will think about them. This fear-based thinking breeds inaction. Ironically, these leaders do a great job gathering important information for good decision making but get bogged down in analysis paralysis. They get stuck.

On the other hand, arrogant leaders take action without thinking through the consequences. They charge ahead with a false confidence in themselves without researching all the information available to them, acting independently instead of consulting others. More often than not, they're oblivious to the thoughts of others. Their predominant thinking is that everything is all about them. Bad decisions and mistrust from others then results. Why would people want to follow a leader who's out for only his or her self-gain?

Confident leaders have the humility to slow down and put things in proper perspective. They seek the truth and prepare for what lies ahead. C. S. Lewis gave us a great definition of humility: "True humility is not thinking less of yourself; it is thinking of yourself less."[1] Jay is a confident and successful leader because his focus is not on himself but on doing what's best for the organization and others. He has the humility to slow down, know the truth, gather the facts, and do the necessary research while also having the confidence to make bold decisions even in the face of uncertainty and naysayers.

Jay possesses two important qualities that confident leaders employ: wisdom and action. Wisdom is a two-part equation. It's not just knowing the right thing to do; it's also doing the right thing. Both wise counsel and courageous action are required. I've known Jay personally and professionally for fifteen years. He's always been humble enough to know he needed wise counsel from trusted peers, and he's always been confident enough to make the bold decision necessary in spite of the uncertainty.

What We're Really Conquering

Life is imperfect and so are we. In my life, circumstances have triggered a wide range of responses. When I was facing recurrent rejections from publishers, lack of confidence stymied me. Then when *God Is My CEO* became a best seller, my ego got the best of me. Jay admitted that before his accident, he was as arrogant as the day was long and he would crush anyone who got in his way. Bottom line, difficulty can bring out the worst in us. We negatively react in so many ways.

On the positive side, our circumstances can be fertile ground for personal change and growth. Difficulties stir in us a potential we never thought we had; they encourage us to overcome. In my case, my humility provided the means to conquer my lack of confidence. My fear of appearing on *The 700 Club* was a catalyst for becoming a confident leader. The situation humbled me to the point that I could overcome my fear.

In Jay's case, his horrific accident gave newfound faith that provided him with a humble heart to lead a life of purpose beyond himself. He applied his leadership for the sake of his family and his organization, and his humility gave him the means to overcome his arrogance. This inner transformation enabled him to transform his life from convict to successful CEO.

We all have a dominant trait for either lack of confidence or overconfidence. In Jay's case it was overconfidence. In mine it was lack of confidence. What's yours? What's the mountain that keeps you stuck? What circumstances keep you from moving forward with confidence?

I love Sir Edmund Hillary's quote: "It is not the mountain we conquer, but ourselves."[2] In all likelihood, the circumstance you're facing is not something you can surmount in three big easy steps. Rather, it's a long journey of many small steps as you conquer the self-limiting thoughts that keep you from realizing your full potential as a leader at work and at home.

Having the humility to put things in proper perspective is an ongoing character trait that will serve you well at all times. It has three key benefits:

1. *Confidence is a skill set that can be learned and developed.* Confidence is a choice. You always have the freedom to make choices, and you have the opportunity to exercise your confidence every day.

2. *Confidence is like having a built-in alarm system.* With humility, you have the ability to recognize when lack of confidence or overconfidence creeps into your psyche. This self-awareness helps regulate your thoughts into a right perspective. That's why having accountability groups is so important. Trusted peers can point out your blind spots and keep you in the right frame of mind.

3. *Confidence establishes precedents.* When you conquer one personal challenge, it sets a precedent for conquering future challenges. As an example, if you have a fear of public speaking yet overcome that fear to give a talk, it makes the second talk easier, then the third, and so on.

Since circumstances constantly change, Jay and I suggest you focus on developing your confidence as a lifelong pursuit.

20

Crossing
Your Jordan River

(Larry)

I've struggled with a lack of confidence my whole life. There have even been times when I've gotten down on myself for being a "chicken." Conquering the mountains in my life has been difficult because it requires that I overcome my own fears and insecurities—so much so that I actually developed an exercise called the "Biblical Hall of Chickens" in my previous book, *God Is My Success: Transforming Adversity into Your Destiny.*

Half in jest and half in seriousness, I created a chart that showed how four great biblical heroes, when called, rationalized why they weren't qualified for God's call to action. I designed the exercise for the benefit of the book's reading audience, but deep down I took comfort that I wasn't the only one to weasel out of God's call. Imagining myself as one of the Israelites who received the news to get ready to cross the Jordan River, I could hear myself rationalizing the wonderful benefits of the desert: *This place isn't so bad. Besides, it's a dry heat!*

I know how difficult it is to take an honest look at yourself, but I encourage you to reflect on the "Biblical Hall of Chickens" and then go through the questions in the discussion guide. Each of the four great leaders identified in this exercise expressed a lack of confidence but took a leap of faith in spite of their fears. By doing so, they impacted countless generations. On a more personal note, both Jay and I experienced our most significant growth when we embraced our greatest challenges with humility and confidence.

We all have a promised land that includes finding and fulfilling our potential. We also have a Jordan River to cross as a rite of passage. Regardless of the size of your mountain or the depth of your river to cross, it is our hope that personal reflection and the discussion guide will provide the necessary wisdom, humility, courage, and confidence for realizing your full potential.

The Biblical Hall of Chickens
The Reluctant Hero: Four Great Biblical Leaders and Their Responses to God's Calling

Biblical Leader	Response to God's Calling	God's Promise
Jeremiah (Jeremiah 1:6–8)	"I do not know how to speak; I am only a child."	"Do not be afraid of them, for I am with you and will rescue you."
Moses (Exodus 4:10–12)	"Lord, I have never been eloquent, neither in the past nor since you have spoken to your servant. I am slow of speech and tongue."	"I will help you speak and will teach you what to say."

Bold Choice 4: Confidence

Biblical Leader	Response to God's Calling	God's Promise
Gideon (Judges 6:14–16)	"But how can I save Israel? My clan is the weakest in Manasseh and I am the least in my family."	"I will be with you, and you will strike down all the Midianites together."
Solomon (I Kings 3:7–12)	"But I am only a little child and do not know how to carry out my duties."	"I will give you a wise and discerning heart."

Discussion Guide

- What is your most dominant tendency? Lack of confidence or overconfidence? During what conditions do these tendencies manifest themselves? Explain.

- Describe a time when you battled with either lack of confidence or overconfidence. What was the outcome?

- Describe a time when negative self-talk impacted your life. How did you overcome this?

- Describe a time when you were confident—when you had the humility to keep things in the proper perspective. What was the result of your humble confidence?

Bold Choice 5:

Balance

Choosing the Harder Right

over the Easier Wrong

We get only one life, and we

certainly don't want to live by default.

Doing nothing or running away

makes us victims of circumstance.

21

Riding the Waves
of Imbalance

(Larry)

In an ideal world, most of us would live a peaceful life of balance. We would love to have our personal, professional, and family lives join together in harmony. However, we don't live in an ideal world. Our world is real and sometimes harsh, with challenging circumstances that hit us in unrelenting waves. Sometimes the waves build slowly and other times they crash into our lives without warning. Regardless of the intensity, they throw us off balance.

As a child who grew up on the south shore of Long Island and an adult who lived by the coast in Southern California, I've spent a good part of my life riding the waves at the beach. In order to ride, I had to learn to rise above the waves or go through them. I also learned the hard way that there are two things you absolutely can't do: You can't stand still in ignorance of the waves, and you can't run away from them in fear back to shore. The waves will knock you down. The ocean, like life, is constantly changing. While changing circumstances can throw us off balance, we can train and equip ourselves to respond effectively in order to steady our footing.

On a macro level, the work/family/life issue is too broad and complex to solve. However, on a micro level as it relates to our life, it's definitely actionable. We start with a couple of simple questions: "What am I going to do about my imbalance when the waves of my circumstances come crashing into my life?" and "How will I respond?"

Speaking from experience, doing nothing or running away are options that put us at risk. We get only one life, and we certainly don't want to live by default. Doing nothing or running away makes us victims of circumstance. The next chapters offer some positive options for you to live a more balanced life—a way to go over the waves of imbalance and a way to go through your circumstances. You'll hear stories from Joel Manby (the CEO of Sea World), Jay, and me, and then we'll share about our imbalance and how we either rose above our situation or persevered through it. In this book's conclusion, I'll offer some suggestions to help you see your imbalance as an opportunity to grow rather than a circumstance to avoid.

22

Making the Hard Choices to Get Back in Balance: Joel Manby's Story

(Larry)

Joel Manby is an American success story. As a young boy, Joel was determined to rise above his circumstances and find prosperity. His dad, owner of a small farm machinery dealership in Battle Creek, Michigan, struggled to keep food on the table. "Growing up without financial means, I didn't want the same financial pressures of my parents," Joel explains. He worked hard, became a straight-A student and graduated from Harvard Business School. As an executive at Saturn Corporation, he helped the startup carmaker go from zero to $5 billion a year in revenue in just three years. His success at Saturn resulted in a promotion to CEO of Saab North America, where he led the division to its second-best year in Saab's North American history.[1]

Despite this success, life wasn't always good for Joel. Here's the flip-side of what happened, in his own words:

My wife, Marki, and I moved ten times in fifteen years as I accepted new leadership positions of increasing responsibility and pressure. The constant moving put a tremendous strain on our home life and our four girls. I spent more than 250 days on the road, mostly in Asia—and even when I was home, I consistently had 6:00 a.m. phone calls with Sweden and 11:00 p.m. phone calls with the Asian markets.

On September 13, 1999, I was in Australia for a Saab distributor meeting and called Marki to catch up. As she started to talk, her voice cracked. "This is the second year in a row you've been away on my birthday. When you're home, you're not really *home*. This is not what I signed up for. I thought I could handle this, and I've tried. But this isn't working for our family. You're frustrated. You're not happy and neither am I. The kids don't really know you. Something needs to change."[2]

Marki's words were a wake-up call. Joel deeply desired to be a good husband and father. So he went to his boss, the CEO of Saab worldwide, to ask if he could return to being CEO of "only" Saab's North American Operations, a move that would cut Joel's travel in half. His boss refused.

Joel made the difficult decision to leave Saab and soon accepted a position as the CEO of a startup company in California. During his first week, the NASDAQ crashed, losing over a third of its value. He began working 24/7 to try to salvage the company, renting an apartment in California and traveling to Atlanta only once or twice a month.

The path he thought would lead him back to his family instead led him to a bare, lonely apartment. One rainy night, depressed and hopeless, Joel wrestled with some serious questions. He asked himself, *My entire career I've been so driven . . . for what? Is there any hope of balancing my career goals with my family goals? Are quarterly profit reports really what life is all about?*[3]

The Rest of the Story

On that eventful rainy night in his apartment, Joel received a phone call from Jack Herschend, chairman of the board of Herschend Family Entertainment Corporation (HFE), which Joel had been on the board of for three years. He thought highly of Jack and the company, and that phone call led Joel to become the chairman and CEO of HFE, one of the largest themed entertainment companies in the world.

As CEO, Joel went on to integrate the core values of agape love as working principles in the organization. He then wrote an excellent leadership book called *Love Works* as a result of his positive experience at HFE. In it he writes of how his work/family balance paradigm changed dramatically:

> All my life I had been living by the numbers because numbers were all my leaders seemed to care about. If I had deeper principles, I needed to check them at the company door, because once I was at work, it was all about financial performance. Inside I longed for a better way—a way to unite who I was as a business leader with who I was as a person. I wanted to work somewhere that rejected the false dichotomy between profit and people or profit and principles. I wanted in short, to be the same person all the time: at work, with my family, at my church, and when I was alone.[4]

Thanks to his perseverance, Joel ended up working for an organization that became highly successful due to the founders' deep-seated core values, ones that honor the importance of integrating family balance into their organization.

Making the harder right choice
over the easier alternative will ultimately
help you realize your potential and
appreciate the journey.

23

Making the Hard Choices to Get Back in Balance: Jay Coughlan's Story

(Jay)

My problem with finding balance was my tendency to go into sixth gear. When I was CEO at Lawson Software, the demands of business were constant. There weren't enough hours in the day to address all of my responsibilities. Some disaster at work would bring me to fifth gear, where I'd be working eighty hours a week. Inevitably, more issues would pile on top, taking me to sixth gear, which meant working at least one hundred hours a week.

The issue was that I could stay in sixth gear, and it felt normal. I would even brag about my workload as if it were a badge of courage. But who was I hurting? Everybody who mattered to me. I was destroying the people around me, and sadly, my family took the brunt of my imbalance. I was destroying my wife. I was destroying my kids and everything else. At work, my employees, peers, and customers were all getting my wrath. In essence, I was demolishing the other priorities I had. It wasn't just away from home; I was neglecting my health, family, friends, and all the energy-producing activities that gave me life.

Things came to a head when Lawson was looking to merge with a Swedish company. The merger would almost double our size from $450 million in revenue to approximately $800 million. In all likelihood, once the merger was finalized I would have to spend even more time away from home as CEO. But as much as I enjoyed the opportunity at Lawson, I knew how much I was needed at home. Jule had her hands full raising three kids while I was absent during this important stage in our family's life.

The beauty of being a goal setter was that I had the discipline to review my goals every three months. It didn't take long for me to see I was out of balance due to my ability to go into sixth gear. The stark realization of my imbalance was sobering, and the alarm in my head sounded off loud and clear: *You've got to get out of sixth gear now! Don't wait twelve months. You've got to get home. You've got to start working out more. You've got to spend time with Jule and the kids. You need to make an adjustment right now!*

The Rest of the Story

Finding balance requires hard choices. I came to the conclusion that to persevere through this challenging time, I needed to be in balance. I also knew that being in balance would make me be a better leader in every area in life—at work and at home. Finding balance was the answer.

I went back to my strength as a goal setter but this time reframed my approach. As I reviewed my goals, I asked myself, *How far out of balance am I? What adjustments do I need to make? What decisions will give me better balance in my life?*

I remember coming home one night and having a moment of clarity. My family was a priority, and the right thing to do was to leave Lawson Software. If I didn't leave, I would be a hypocrite to the goal of having my family a priority.

I went to the board and told them I would honor my commitment to get the merger done, but I wasn't going to stay on as CEO. I received a lot of pressure to stay, even from my financial advisor, who told me I'd be leaving a lot of money on the table. It was tough to leave, but looking back it was definitely the right thing to do. In the months and years that followed, our family grew closer. I had a great time with the kids during an important time in their lives. Jule and I grew closer. If I'd stayed with that job, I would have had a great career, but I'm certain my family wouldn't be what it is today.

Now I have the opportunity to coach leaders and businesspeople from all walks of life. I've found that most are stuck in some work or family issue primarily because they're out of balance—a dangerous place to be. They're expending huge amounts of time and energy spinning their wheels but not getting out of the ditch. I try to help them see the big picture that their life is a marathon and not a sprint. The first thing I do is to have them go through my 168-hour test. An entire week comprises 168 hours, and it's one of the few things in life that are fair.

When I coach people with the 168 Rule, I start by asking them to list all the things they like to do that give them energy—things like: walk the dog, spend time with family, go skiing, or go to dinner with friends.

Then I ask them how many hours per day they sleep. Let's say the answer is seven hours per day. We then multiply times seven days to get forty-nine, which rounds up to fifty hours. Then I ask how many hours per week they work. Let's say the answer is fifty hours. The total has reached one hundred hours, which leaves sixty-eight hours remaining. I ask more questions: "How often do you watch TV? How much time do you spend on the computer? How long is your commute?" Soon people realize that if they don't have clarity on their waking hours and don't prioritize them, their time slips away pretty quickly.

Ultimately, I try to help them take charge of their lives by taking charge of their mind. I help them see the reality of their imbalance in order to find true balance. If they don't have clarity, prioritize what matters, and build a plan and take action, they will remain stuck. Balance helps them persevere and enjoy the journey. It's not letting the misery of the moment keep them down and instead finding the strategies and actions that lift them back up.

Here's the hard truth: Life is ever changing, and there will always be times in our life when we will be out of balance. I created the five bold choices as a vehicle for helping people get unstuck. It's not a static five-step process that ends with balance as the ultimate goal; it's a vehicle that helps you appreciate the journey and realize your potential.

I would view the five bold choices as circular rather than as a linear process ending at balance. When you're imbalanced, you need to go back to finding clarity. When I was out of balance in sixth gear, I had to stop and review my goals by asking the difficult questions: *How far out of balance am I? What adjustments will I make? What decisions do I need to make to find better balance in my life? How can I enjoy life in spite of my difficulties?*

As tough as it is to ask these questions, it's even harder to act on them by making the needed choices. However, in the end, making the harder right choice over the easier alternative will ultimately help you realize your potential and appreciate the journey.

When things are challenging and
we're out of balance, we're in danger—
not so much from the circumstances
but from our own thoughts.

24

Making the Hard Choices to Get Back in Balance: Larry Julian's Story

(Larry)

My heart sank and my body ached as the sonographer continued her vain search for a beating heart. She finally turned to my wife and me and said, "I'm sorry." After a brief conversation, she left the room. Sherri and I were left in a dark room, staring at the screen showing our unborn child in stunned silence.

Before then, my life had already been out of balance as I battled the fatigue and discouragement of constant book rejections—but Sherri and I had at least held onto the promise of starting a family. Now, the devastating news sent my thoughts to a dark, dark place. I was angry, hurting, frustrated, and stunned. Honestly, I wanted to quit all work and run away from everything. To make matters worse, I had a business trip coming up soon. As much as I wanted to cancel, I had to honor my commitment to the organization that had planned the event for over six months.

Two weeks later I flew to Bend, Oregon, to conduct a two-day business seminar. The first day was a challenge. I struggled to get my head in the right frame of mind. On the second day, I had a free morning before I was scheduled to conduct an afternoon program, so I went on a hike to clear my head. I would take in some beautiful scenery for a couple of hours and come back refreshed for my afternoon program. The front-desk clerk at our resort recommended Mount Bachelor, and I jumped in my rental car and drove to the hiking trail about thirty minutes away.

I parked the car in the lot adjacent to the start of the trail, which had a posted mileage of about four miles. I thought to myself, *I'm in good shape. I can do that!* A quick calculation assured me I could hike it in a few hours and be back in plenty of time. My car was the only one in the lot, so I would enjoy the solitude.

The first part of the hike was beautiful. At around 10:30 a.m., the weather was perfect for hiking—a cool seventy-eight degrees. An hour later, the trail left the cool, shaded canopy of trees and began its path through a barren, sun-parched landscape of black jagged rock. The temperature shot up into the nineties. Because the landscape was all rock, the trail became less distinct and I started to become disoriented. Until this point the hiking had been easy because it was primarily downhill in the shade, but now it became a rigorous uphill climb in the hot midday sun with no breeze at all. I was ill-prepared for what I thought would be a simple hike to clear my head. The one twelve-ounce bottle of water I had brought was now half empty and my only food was a half-eaten granola bar.

What I didn't know but learned later was that Mount Bachelor is an extinct volcano. This particular hike called for a descent into the black and barren pit of the volcano followed by a steep climb back up. As I continued to make the uphill climb, I became tired and overheated. There was no shade or breeze to cool me off. I started to worry.

Am I still on the path? Maybe I should go back the way I came. My thoughts quickly shifted to fear mode. *I'm lost! What if I run out of water?* Within minutes, I was angry with myself. *I'm an idiot! Why did I come here in the first place? What was I thinking?* Finally, full panic set in. *I'm going to die out here!* My heart raced, I sweated profusely, and I felt dizzy as if I might pass out.

The Rest of the Story

Panic is a terrifying, nauseating feeling. My thoughts were like a runaway freight train. I knew I had to corral them quickly, because if I didn't I would be in serious danger. I sat down and prayed for guidance and was eventually able to calm down enough to bring my thoughts under control.

Ironically, as I tell this story today, I see how I used much of Jay's application of the five choices. I gained clarity on the truth by calmly walking myself through the facts to determine whether to stay on the trail to its destination or go back. I decided to continue on toward my destination. I adapted by deciding to ration my remaining water and granola bar. I developed more confidence by putting things in proper perspective. I calmed down enough to rid myself of the panic that I was going to die. I now had a plan and action steps to take, and my frame of mind gave me enough balance to move forward and keep my brain in check even in a frightening situation.

After a couple of hours of arduous hiking, I saw a sign that read "Parking Lot—Half Mile." In my mind, the sign read, *Congratulations, you're not going to die!* I continued to climb, and the barren rock became an open path that led me to a spectacular panoramic vista that included a beautiful blue lake and lush green trees. This seemed as close to dying and going to heaven as I could imagine. It reminded me of the scene in *The Wizard of Oz* when Dorothy steps out of her home after it lands in Oz and everything goes from black and white to full color.

As I ascended farther I heard the *whoosh* of trees, and then a cool, pine-scented breeze provided cooling for my sweat-soaked body. At the end of the trail was a bench under a shady tree. I sat down and savored the last bite of my granola bar and then quenched my thirst with the remaining water. I even had twenty minutes to sit under the tree and find some peace after enduring the turbulence in my head. It was almost as if God provided this special moment to help me put things in proper perspective even when the world seemed like it was caving in on me.

When things are challenging and we're out of balance, we're in danger—not so much from the circumstances but from our own thoughts. As I looked back on that experience now, I realize that I had to literally and figuratively rise above my circumstances to overcome the danger before me. I had been alone, but I did feel like I had help. My peace of mind, proper perspective, faith, and perseverance sustained me. Sir Edmund Hillary was right. We need to conquer ourselves before we can conquer our mountains.

I made it back to the conference in time and was able to continue my leadership training. But this time, my program was distinctly different from the one the day before. Many people came up to me afterward and told me how impactful my presentation was. On reflection of my program, I don't think the content or delivery changed, but I do believe I developed a more balanced perspective that changed me for the better.

Even so, this one event didn't change my circumstances back home in Minneapolis. My wife and I still walked a long road before we had our first child, and years of rejection preceded the publishing of *God Is My CEO*. However, my crazy hiking experience was a small but powerful precedent for helping me find a more balanced perspective. As I look back on that time in my life, I see that this balanced perspective helped me become a better person, which over time made me a better husband, father, and leader.

The work/family/life balance issue

is an equal-opportunity

thorn in the flesh of most workers.

It doesn't discriminate.

25

From Chaos to Calm

(Larry)

Jay and Joel are both examples of leaders who were able to transcend their work/family/life balance issue and in the process bring their leadership to a higher level. They redefined leadership as an integrated whole life rather than a compartmentalized and fragmented life.

Prior to Jay and Joel finding balance, the imbalance in their lives not only negatively impacted them, but they themselves also had a negative impact—on the people around them, particularly their families. Both men are extremely bright, competent, and gifted CEOs as well as men of deep faith and character who love their families.

So how do leaders of their caliber get so out of balance? Do they have a weakness? A character flaw? Not at all. They, like all of us who love and value family, simply suffered under the pressure of trying to work hard and provide financially while being a fully engaged spouse, parent, and family member.

The work/family/life balance issue is an equal-opportunity thorn in the flesh of most workers. It doesn't discriminate. Whether we're an executive, an entry-level worker, a doctor, a student, or a stay-at-home mom, the pull of opposing forces can easily throw life off balance. What matters lies in how we see the issue and what we do about it.

When I think of today's work/family/life balance dilemma, I'm reminded of the old vaudeville act of the juggler trying to spin several plates on top of long, thin sticks all at the same time. The background is set by loud, fast-paced music, and the juggler frantically moves from plate to plate to keep each one spinning. The audience sits anxiously on the edge of their seats in anticipation of the first plate that will fall. The tension builds as the juggler tries in vain before all the plates wobble and crash to the ground one by one.

While this juggling act is entertaining to watch, it's a different story when we're trying to balance competing priorities in real life. Sadly, I think many buy into the paradigm that their lives are compartmentalized into several spinning plates that must be juggled in order to find life balance. Think for a moment how stressed we get when we're trying to decide which urgent priority to address when several others also demand our undivided attention. For me, it creates a tornado of negative thoughts and emotions that spins out mental debris of guilt and frustration when one plate of life comes crashing down at the expense of another. If we're not careful, all the plates can come down.

I would like to offer another paradigm. Picture a tightrope walker. In all likelihood this person has a significant understanding of the laws of balance as well as years of core training in mind, body, and spirit. This training enables the tightrope walker to safely cross from point A to point B without falling into a chasm of harm, and the process puts the entire balancing act within the heart and mind. The tightrope walker is grounded and focused on a desired destination, using a pole as an aid to balance two opposing forces.

Here's a quote from acrobat Nik Wallenda after his walk across the Grand Canyon on a tightrope: "You can go into a haunted house and be completely calm—'Hey, this is just a gimmick'—or you can be scared to death. It's wherever you let your mind go." He continues, "I've learned through struggles, even in my marriage, that man, your mind is powerful. That's a key to living life in general, not just walking the wire."[1] In an interview with *Christianity Today* he says, "So many people lose their dreams because someone in their life or they … talk themselves out of it. I hope what people see me do inspires them to believe nothing is impossible."[2]

I love Nik's mind-set. Clearly he has balanced his mind-set to the point of functioning well in less than ideal circumstances. If Nik can walk a tightrope across the Grand Canyon, and leaders like Jay and Joel can reframe their paradigm on work and faith, I believe we can find balance too. I believe we have the capacity to transcend whatever keeps us stuck.

Regardless of what we've done

in the past or where we are at present,

we have the privilege to determine

the rest of the story.

26

The Rest of the Story

(Larry)

One of my greatest revelations about balance came while I was watching a video of planet earth taken from space. It showed how the weather patterns all together make up a perfectly balanced life in motion. How awe-inspiring to witness a planet in perfect balance and harmony.

However, those of us living down here on earth can see only the imbalance and turbulence of weather that affects our immediate life. We can't see the big picture from above, only the constant turmoil of storms rolling through.

On that day on Mount Bachelor, I was convinced that I was stuck in a bad situation. My choices were to remain frozen in fear in the dangerous heat or to run back to my point of origin. Both were reactive based on the perceived circumstances in front of me. In reality, there was a spectacular place waiting for me when I got past my circumstances and continued my journey. Sometimes we just need to trust in the unseen.

We also need to trust in the gifts of peace, perspective, and perseverance that God places within us. Bottom line, we have the power and capacity to rise above our challenges. Sometimes it's within our own power to rise above, while other times we need to be lifted up. Either way, we can transcend our circumstances and triumph over our trials.

Perhaps you noticed the "The Rest of the Story" heading at the end of the stories that Jay, Joel, and I shared. The idea came from a famous radio announcer named Paul Harvey, who shared stories of interesting people and celebrities. He would hold back key elements or defining moments that determined the outcome of the story and then reveal them at the end and sign off by stating, "And now you know the rest of the story."

What I love most about having faith in God is knowing that he gives us the tools to define our success and the freedom to make the choices that determine our destiny. Regardless of what we've done in the past or where we are at present, we have the privilege to determine the rest of the story.

What is the rest of your story? In what ways are your present choices determining your future outcomes? It is our hope and prayer that you continue to trust in the unseen even when life seems out of balance. Regardless of your circumstances, choose the harder right path over the easier wrong one. We believe your hope and perseverance will lead you to define—and refine—the rest of your story.

Discussion Guide

- Describe a time when you felt out of balance. What caused the imbalance?

- Describe a time when you were torn between work and family obligations. What did you do to rectify the situation?

- What actions do you take when you feel your life getting out of balance?

- What bold choices would you make to live a more balanced life?

Appreciating the Journey

Appreciation is both a gift

and a discipline. But if it's

not exercised every day,

you risk losing it.

27

Appreciating the Value of Your Journey

(Larry)

Appreciation has three distinct meanings rolled into a powerful gift. It means:

1. To be fully aware of the "significance" or "magnitude" of something or someone.

2. An "expression of gratitude" for something or someone.

3. Something that raises in "value or price, especially over time" like a work of art.[1]

Appreciating your journey means:

1. You're able to discern the hidden value and significance of each circumstance no matter how difficult. Appreciation acts as a filter that keeps negative thinking from infiltrating

your mind. It also acts as a magnifying glass that heightens your self-awareness, other awareness, and circumstance awareness.

2. You enjoy your journey. You're grateful for your circumstances, even the challenging ones. Appreciation gives you the ability to be thankful and joyful in all circumstances, good and bad.

3. You make bold choices that raise the value of your journey, as a result of wisdom gained. Appreciation helps you find and realize your potential, and it taps into your inherent ability or capacity for growth, development, and becoming the extremely valuable person God designed you to be. When you appreciate your journey, your life grows in value over time. Your growth benefits others around you, and your journey makes a difference in the world.

Appreciation is both a gift and a discipline. But if it's not exercised every day, you risk losing it. Think of the phrase "use it or lose it" with regard to exercise. Daily exercise builds your muscles; if you don't exercise, your muscles will atrophy. In the same way, if you don't exercise your gift of appreciation, your mind will be prone to negative thinking. Your attitude shifts from positive to negative. If you don't appreciate your journey, it will stall and become stagnant.

God doesn't create shoddy work. When he made you, he created a uniquely gifted individual to make the world a better place. It starts with you—with not only recognizing your value but also appreciating the journey to finding and fulfilling your potential. You've been blessed with the freedom to choose. It's our hope that you joyfully accept the challenge of appreciating your journey. Not only will you benefit, but so will everyone around you.

Let's reflect on Jay's lessons learned, and then I'll close with some final thoughts.

I realize I'm not entitled to anything,

yet I've received blessings regardless

of whether I deserve them or not.

28

Appreciating the Second Chance at Life

(Jay)

The purpose of sharing my story in this book came about when someone approached me after one of my speeches and asked, "How is it that you were so successful despite the circumstances you went through after your accident?" The question forced me to think back and determine what, in addition to my faith, had allowed me to persevere and find my true potential.

In reflecting on that, I've come to realize that the real treasure was in appreciating the journey along the way, not in some perfect destination that can never be reached. My life was a roller-coaster ride after my accident. Most of the early days were filled with pain, stress, and difficulty as I balanced recovery, jail time, and keeping my career afloat. To enjoy the journey, I had to develop an unwavering commitment to find balance in my life. My five bold choices to find clarity, accountability, adaptability, confidence, and balance all contributed to overcoming the most challenging period of my life.

Having a more balanced state of mind gave me a better perspective on life, providing greater awareness of my surroundings. It also helped me gain more understanding of who I am and who I want to be as a person, father, husband, and leader. In it I found a greater perception of the truth, not the negative self-talk that kept me up at night.

The balance I gained gave me the wisdom and courage to make the bold, right choices during the chaotic times. Ultimately, during the most challenging of times, I was able to appreciate and even enjoy the journey. I didn't allow the misery of the moment to keep me down and instead found strategies and actions to lift me back up.

Life isn't fair or easy, but it can be fun and exciting. From celebrating achievements to learning from failures to surrounding myself with energy-giving people, I've always had a strategy to enjoy the journey. In the most difficult times, I developed a greater appreciation of my family, my friends, and life in general in spite of everything.

As I look back on my life, I'm deeply thankful that in spite of my terrible mistake, I've been forgiven by God and my family. I've been given a second chance. I realize I'm not entitled to anything, yet I've received blessings regardless of whether I deserve them or not. When I was in the emergency room at Hennepin County Hospital, broken into pieces and staring into the abyss, I wasn't thinking about my boat. I was appreciating what's most important: my wife, my dad, my mom, and my kids.

We will always have highs and lows on our journey through life. However, appreciating the journey through the ups and downs will help us realize our full potential of serving others and making the world a better place.

Do you appreciate your journey in spite of the difficult circumstances you're in? Do you have a clear sense of who you are and where you're going? Where do you go for wisdom, direction, peace, and support? Are you aware of the impact you have on others?

These are some tough self-reflection questions to ask, but they're also extremely important. The answers, whether big and small, provide opportunities to discover your true courage. You need to be the one to search out the truth and take charge of your personal growth. Your courageous action will benefit not only you but also those around you.

Pain and suffering are part

of life—they require a response,

and how we respond will determine

the trajectory of our life.

29

Appreciation Focuses on What We Have Rather Than What We Don't Have

(Larry)

I place significant emphasis on being aware of bold choices. Often, these defining moments are times when my self-reflection reveals the hidden flaws of pride. With this in mind, I think of one specific incident that changed my life forever.

Twenty-five years ago I was hired by an executive director named Lamar who started a ministry to help corporate CEOs integrate their work and faith. My job was to facilitate CEO discussion groups in Minneapolis. I loved everything about facilitating these groups, and deep down, I also loved the power and prestige that went with the position.

One day Lamar came up to me and said, "I would like to facilitate these groups and have you take notes." I was indignant. The change felt like a demotion and I almost quit, but after some reflection I recognized that my pride was getting in the way of an important service to leaders. I then came to the realization that I still had a wonderful opportunity, just in a different role. So I reluctantly took the job of note taker.

Talk about blessing in disguise. This one decision changed my life forever. In essence, I humbly became a fly on the wall and listened to the leaders' deep conversations. Months later I had the revelation that these leaders struggled to follow God's principles in a bottom-line world. I thought to myself, *These leaders can pray to God on Sunday but have to check God at the door Monday through Friday.* That one thought led to my calling to write *God Is My CEO.* It all started with self-awareness of my pride, which then provided the humility to listen and also gave me an appreciation for the privilege of hearing the transparent discussions of CEOs. Appreciation resulted in my inspiration to write a book.

If we go back through the five bold choices that Jay made, we'll see the role that awareness and appreciation had in every aspect of his journey from convict to CEO. In the clarity chapter, he helped us discern how to prioritize our activities and goals. In the accountability chapter, he provided an invaluable way to debrief our successes and failures so we can improve. In the adaptability chapter, he shared how his passion for continuous learning helped him adapt to change. In the confidence chapter, he conveyed how knowing the truth was key to making important decisions. And in the balance chapter, he demonstrated his courageous self-examination when he realized that he needed to quit his CEO position to spend more time with his family. In every facet of his life, Jay put a premium on awareness and appreciation.

His advice has helped me relive and revive the depth and meaning of appreciation in life. Back in the winter of 2009, I came out with my third book, titled *God Is My Coach: A Business Leaders Guide to Finding Clarity in an Uncertain World*, which included a chapter on appreciation. After the book's release, the publisher sent me on a radio tour throughout the country. I broke the book down into "talking points"—short key themes—and one was the title of this chapter: "Appreciation helps us focus on what we have rather than what we don't have."

During the time of the radio tour, the country was in the midst of a financial crisis, with a high unemployment rate. Normally, the radio announcers who conducted the interviews were supportive, but on one particular show the host blasted my point as some positive-thinking Pollyanna platitude. She ranted how some of her friends had lost their jobs and others had lost their homes, then blurted out, "Why should we appreciate what we have when we're suffering with all that we lost?" I tried to articulate my point, but she quickly shut down the interview.

Two weeks later I flew to Philadelphia to conduct a weekend seminar on my book. In it, I dedicated a good amount of time to the topic of appreciation. The men in this group embraced my thesis on appreciation, and we had a good hour of interaction with lots of great feedback.

After the seminar, the leader of the group, John, a quiet man in his sixties, offered to drive me back to the airport. On the way, I commented about how animated the group became when I broached the theme of appreciating what we have rather focusing on what we don't have.

A long awkward silence followed, then he said, "I lost my wife to cancer several years back. She was the love of my life. I was blessed with a wonderful marriage of thirty-five years. After she died, I went through a long period of grief when I just couldn't get past my loss. Every night I would visit her grave and just sob. In my prayers, I would constantly ask God why. Then one evening I came to a revelation that changed my life.

"I remember thinking to myself, I've been coaching men for years who've shared painful stories of broken relationships with their wives. I've witnessed men go through years of brokenness and divorce. Then it hit me. God blessed me with a thirty-five-year marriage to a wonderful woman. What a wonderful gift from God! My grief melted into gratitude. My mind-set shifted completely and I started to appreciate life again. A few years later I met my second wife, who had also lost her spouse to cancer. Our marriage is going great."

When I asked John why his second marriage was doing well, he answered, "We don't sweat the small stuff. We both recognize the value of marriage. We're able to appreciate each other's positive qualities, and we don't let the small stuff get in our way. Our marriage and our remaining time on earth are too precious to waste on trivial things."

Through the radio host's indignant response and John's poignant comments, I've come to see just how powerful appreciation is. I understand the host's outrage (after all, it is difficult to appreciate life in the face of tragic events like losing a job, losing a loved one, dealing with an illness, or going through hardship), but pain and suffering are part of life—they require a response, and how we respond will determine the trajectory of our life. Here are a few quotes from leaders who suffered greatly yet expressed their appreciation through their lives.[1]

What We Have Rather Than What We Don't Have

The best way to show my gratitude to God is to accept everything, even my problems, with joy.

—Mother Teresa, who was plagued with poor health such as heart problems, pneumonia, and malaria

It is only with gratitude that life becomes rich.

—Dietrich Bonhoeffer, who courageously opposed Nazism and Hitler's anti-Semitic policies and spent years in prisons and concentration camps until he was executed by hanging

I thank God for my handicaps; for through them, I have found myself, my work, and my God.

—Helen Keller, who was deaf, mute, and blind

It has seemed to me fit and proper that (the gifts of God) should be solemnly, reverently, and gratefully acknowledged with one heart and voice by the whole American people. I do therefore invite my fellow citizens … to set apart and observe the last Thursday of November next, as a day of Thanksgiving and praise to our beneficent Father who dwelleth in the Heavens.

—Thanksgiving Proclamation by Abraham Lincoln, who led America through one of its most difficult times while beset by depression

Even though surrounded by poverty, unjustly imprisoned, severely handicapped, or facing uncertainty and adversity, these four people lived joy-filled lives of gratitude. If asked what I think is so different about them, I'd say it's their appreciation.

Appreciation is both a gift to receive and an expression of gratitude to share with others. It's the ultimate win-win. We benefit by receiving it, and we benefit others by sharing it.

177

The very difficulty before you is the portal of your significance, and the bold choices you make now in these tough times will determine your better tomorrow.

30

Your Bold Choices Determine Your Destiny

(Larry)

In the words of Oswald Chambers, "All efforts of worth and excellence are difficult. Difficulty does not make us faint and cave in—it stirs us to overcome. God does not give us overcoming life—He gives us life as we overcome."[1]

Jay and I understand being stuck, getting out of balance, and dealing with pain and difficulty. We respect the natural emotions you may be experiencing and understand the challenges you face. That said, we urge you to focus on and appreciate the many gifts you have right now.

It is our prayer that this book has helped you reframe your problems as opportunities. We hope it stirs you to overcome whatever stands between you and your potential, and sincerely believe that you have an untapped God-given potential inside you that's just waiting to manifest into a powerful journey.

The very difficulty before you is the portal of your significance, and the bold choices you make now in these tough times will determine your better tomorrow. Your journey is extremely valuable to God and others. It has worth that will appreciate over time. Others will be blessed because of your perseverance, so make it count for all its worth.

We wish you continued blessings on your journey.

Discussion Guide

- How would you rate your level of appreciation? Why did you give yourself that rating?

- How would you rate your level of self-awareness? Other awareness? Circumstance awareness? God awareness?

- Of the four areas of awareness, which one do you need to improve the most?

- What does "appreciating the journey" mean to you?

- What one or two action steps can you take to help you appreciate your journey more?

Notes

Chapter 1

1   Theodore Roosevelt, goodreads, http://www.goodreads.com/quotes/34690-people-don-t-care-how-much-you-know-until-they-know.

Chapter 2

1   Larry Julian, *God Is My Success: Transforming Adversity into Your Destiny* (New York: Warner Faith, 2005), 28–31.

2   *Unforgiven*, directed by Clint Eastwood (Burbank, CA: Warner Bros., 1992).

Chapter 4

1   *A Few Good Men*, directed by Rob Reiner (Beverly Hills, CA: Castle Rock Entertainment, 1992).

Chapter 5

1   Larry Julian, *God is My CEO: Following God's Principles in a Bottom Line World,* 2nd ed. (Avon, MA: Adams Media, 2014), 236.

Chapter 6

1   Winston Churchill, goodreads, http://www.goodreads.com/quotes/407062-you-will-never-reach-your-destination-if-you-stop-and.

2   John Wooden, goodreads, http://www.goodreads.com/quotes/47570-don-t-mistake-activity-with-achievement.

Chapter 7

1   As cited in Larry Julian, *God Is My Coach: A Business Leaders Guide to Finding Clarity in an Uncertain World* (New York: Center Street, 2009), xvi–xvii.

2   Ralph Waldo Emerson, *Journals and Miscellaneous Notebooks 4:86*, Reading Ralph Waldo Emerson, http://www.readingemerson.com/2011/06/15/it-is-the-storm-within-which-endangers-him-not-the-storm-without/.

Notes

3 Julian, *God Is My CEO*, 183.
4 S. Truett Cathy, *It's Easier to Succeed Than to Fail* (Nashville: Oliver-Nelson Books, 1989), 70.
5 Julian, *God is My CEO*, 185–186.

Chapter 8

1 *Apollo 13*, directed by Ron Howard (Beverly Hills, CA: Imagine Entertainment, 1995).

Chapter 9

1 Jennifer Jones, "Fear of Failure Prompts Workers to Shirk Responsibility," *American Management Association*, September 9, 2013, http://www.amanet.org/9206.aspx.

Chapter 11

1 F. Scott Fitzgerald, goodreads, http://www.goodreads.com/ quotes/96713-never-confuse-a-single-defeat-with-a-final-defeat.

Chapter 12

1 Jim McKay, *ABC's Wide World of Sports* (New York, NY: ABC, 1961-1998).
2 Rochelle Olson, "Vikings kicker Blair Walsh tells first-graders he'll 'cherish' their cards forever," *StarTribune*, January 15, 2016, http://www.startribune.com/vikings-kicker-blair-walsh-meets-blaine-first-graders-who-sent-him-cards/365296091/.

Chapter 13

1 Pink Floyd, "Comfortably Numb," on *The Wall*, PINK-FLOYD-LYRICS.COM, http://www.pink-floyd-lyrics.com/html/comfortably-numb-wall-lyrics.html.

Chapter 14

1 Leon C. Magginson, goodreads, http://www.goodreads.com/ quotes/18875-it-is-not-the-strongest-of-the-species-that-survives.

Chapter 16

1 Leo Tolstoy, goodreads, http://www.goodreads.com/ quotes/12841-everyone-thinks-of-changing-the-world-but-no-one-thinks.

Chapter 18

1 Julian, *God Is My Success*, 84–85.
2 Ibid., 101–102.

Chapter 19

1 C. S. Lewis, goodreads, http://www.goodreads.com/quotes/201236-true-humility -is-not-thinking-less-of-yourself-it-is.

2 Edmund Hillary, goodreads, http://www.goodreads.com/
   quotes/12534-it-is-not-the-mountain-we-conquer-but-ourselves.

Chapter 24

1 Julian, *God is My CEO*, 155.
2 Joel Manby, *Love Works: Seven Timeless Principles for Effective Leaders* (Grand Rapids,
   MI: Zondervan, 2012), 18–19.
3 Ibid., 20.
4 Ibid., 21.

Chapter 26

1 James Sullivan, "Nik Wallenda, Tightrope Walking the Grand Canyon," *Men's
   Journal*, June 10, 2013, http://www.mensjournal.com/adventure/outdoor/
   tightrope-walking-the-grand-canyon-20130610.
2 Allison J. Althoff, "Nik Wallenda's Walk by Faith Across a Grand Canyon Tightrope,"
   Christianity Today, June 21, 2013, http://www.christianitytoday.com/ct/2013/june-web
   -only/walking-by-faith-across-grand-canyon-tightrope.html.

Chapter 28

1 *American Heritage® Dictionary of the English Language,* 5th ed., "Appreciate," http://
   www.thefreedictionary.com/appreciation.

Chapter 29

1 The following quotations are cited in Julian, *God Is My Coach*, 43.

Chapter Chapter 30

1 Oswald Chambers, ed. James G. Reimann, My Utmost for His Highest (Grand Rapids,
   MI: Discovery House Publishers, 1992), July 7 devotional.

Acknowledgments

Jay Coughlan

Larry Julian, thanks for making a laborious process fun.

Scott Meyers, thanks for your insight, wisdom, marketing wizardry, and view of life that, although contrarian at times, is real world and hilarious.

Amy Gardner, thanks for helping me get organized. Without your help, I couldn't have gotten any momentum and would have thrown all my technology in the lake.

Mike Coughlan, thanks for helping me appreciate the journey. Your counsel has been well intentioned, unique, perceptive, entertaining, and occasionally helpful. But mainly, you have always been there for me.

Friends, the source for my material, thanks for motivating me to write it even though you won't read it.

Larry Julian

To my friend Jay Coughlan, who trusted me with telling his remarkable story. It's been an honor to collaborate with you.

To Carlton Garborg and David Sluka at BroadStreet Publishing for making this book a reality.

Special thanks to my family, especially my wife, Sherri, and my children, Grace and Scott, who allow me to experience God's love every day.

My heartfelt appreciation also goes out to Scott and Judy Hackett, Matt and Lolly Pisoni, and Steve and Lesley Hackett.

My gratitude runs deep to friends who inspire me by boldly living their faith in the business world: Dean Bachelor, Jay Bennett, Marc Belton, Ward Brehm, John Busacker, Dennis Doyle, Gordy Engel, Art Erickson, David Frauenshuh, Jim Green, Os Guinness, Bill Hardman, Brad Hewitt, Ron James, Ken Melrose, Al Prentice, Mike Sime, Rob Stevenson, Phil Styrlund, Tad Piper, and Al Quie.

To The Leadership Roundtable members, past and present, who humbly seek to grow as leaders so they can honor God and serve others.

To the Emerging Leader Roundtable members, who give me hope in a next generation of leaders who have a sincere desire to lead with faith and character.

To Dan Rust, author of *Workplace Poker*; Steve Waller, who supplied much-needed diversions; and Jim Walter and John Zappala for their lifelong friendship.

To the National Prayer Breakfast Business Leader Forum team, who reflect the term "Jesus plus nothing" and who've taught me how to help diverse parties meet under the name and person of Jesus.

To those whose daily presence has been lost but whose impact on my life will never be forgotten: Monty Sholund, Stan Geyer, Marty Sinacore, and my mom and dad.

Finally, to my Lord Jesus Christ, thank you for bringing all these people into my life to help me grow closer to you that I might be an instrument for your noble purpose.

About the Authors

Jay Coughlan

Jay Coughlan is a confident and inspiring leader who fosters a culture of high integrity and openness, having served as CEO of such industry leaders as Lawson Software and XRS Corporation. During his tenure as CEO of Lawson Software, the company completed a $200 million IPO while growing revenue from $200 million to $430 million.

Jay has built a national reputation as a keynote speaker, CEO, and mentor to aspiring business leaders. He also is a convicted felon who has spent time in prison. During this dark part of his life, he began developing a framework for dealing with the troubles that life inevitably brings. He uses lessons from his own missteps to help change the paths of individuals and organizations.

Jay is an active regional business advocate and has served on the board of directors for several businesses, currently being board chairman of nonprofit Minnesota Adult and Teen Challenge. He holds a bachelor of science degree in business administration from Bloomsburg University of Pennsylvania. He has been married to his wife, Jule, since 1987, and they have three children and currently reside in Eden Prairie.

Jay's story is one of hope, motivation, personal growth, faith, and forgiveness. He shares how to overcome difficult circumstances and puts people on a journey to have their choices define their life.

Visit *trubalanced.com* for more information.

About the Authors

Larry Julian

Larry Julian is a best-selling author, speaker, and executive coach with over two decades of experience helping CEOs, entrepreneurs, and small business owners successfully lead with their faith and values. As a business coach, he helps leaders transcend challenging situations and succeed in the midst of difficulty. His passion is to help businesspeople overcome the dilemmas that keep them from experiencing the success God intended.

Larry is founder of The Leadership Roundtable, a group of senior executives who meet monthly to discuss issues relevant to work, faith, and family. He has recently formed the Emerging Leader Roundtable for aspiring next-generation leaders. By transforming God's timeless wisdom into daily practical application, Roundtable members grow and impact their immediate spheres of influence in a wide range of industries.

Larry's work has been featured in numerous publications, including the *Wall Street Journal*, *Inc.* magazine, *CNN.com*, and *Fortune* magazine. He has also appeared on *The 700 Club* and *The Tavis Smiley Show*. In addition to *God Is My CEO*, Larry's business leadership books include *God Is My Coach: A Business Leader's Guide to Finding Clarity in an Uncertain World* and *God is My Success: Transforming Adversity into Your Destiny*.

Larry lives in Minneapolis with his wife, Sherri, and their two children.

Visit *larryjulian.com* for more information.

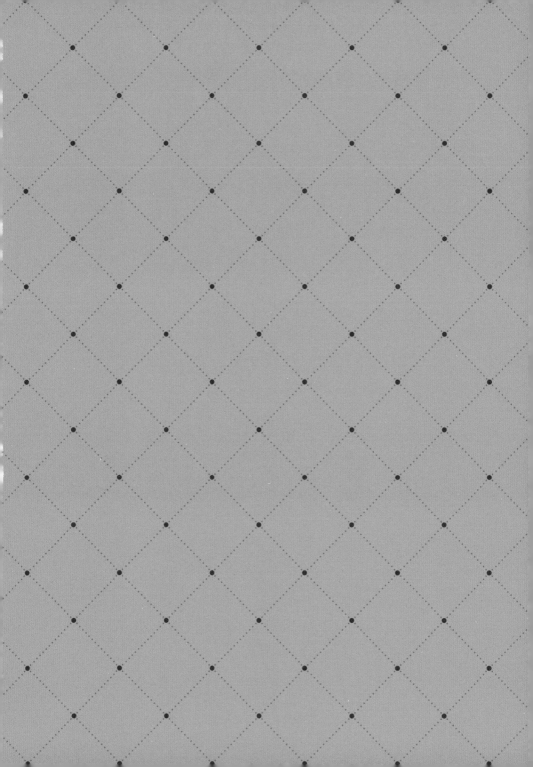